Mak
difference
at Key Stage 3

Learning from five successful schools

Stevie Upton

Contents

Foreword

For the past eighteen months, the Institute of Welsh Affairs has been conducting research into good practice at Key Stage 3 to explore whether recommendations could be made on raising performance in the Welsh secondary system. Key Stage 3 is a critical time in any child's education. It forms the basis for outcomes at GCSE and in the OECD's international Programme for International Student Assessment (PISA) tests. The apparently sharp drop-off in attainment at Key Stage 3 (as compared with Key Stage 2 attainment) that has been occurring for many years is therefore of particular concern. It was this that prompted the research.

Our aim was to undertake research that could generate practical lessons about how to deliver on the key variables that contribute to outstanding performance at Key Stage 3. This detailed focus on Key Stage 3 is one that has not previously been applied in Wales. We hope that the in-depth case studies, coupled with a synthesis of the key features, will provide practitioners and policy makers with a new level of information about good practice in Welsh schools.

Although the research commenced prior to the release of the latest PISA results, it has proved particularly timely in light of Wales' performance. The results show Wales to be performing less well than England, Northern Ireland and Scotland, and below the OECD average; and to be falling further behind. These results have been a shock to the system and the minister – Leighton Andrews – has wasted no time in developing a policy response.

We have found ourselves well placed to make a number of evidence-based responses to these proposed education reforms. The proposals rightly recognise that greater accountability will be needed if all schools are to perform as well as our best. Indeed, our research shows that successful schools are ones that have taken the initiative in employing their own rigorous evaluation and development planning procedures. However, they also display an openness to experimentation which enables the ongoing development of internal capacity and hence generates sustainable success.

We see it as essential that this balance between accountability and adaptability be achieved across the system as a whole and recommend that this principle be adopted as a key policy commitment.

We wish to express our deep gratitude to those without whose support the project would not have been possible. The research was funded by a grant from the Esmée Fairbairn Foundation. The contextual value-added data used in the first phase of the research were supplied by the Welsh Government.

Advice was given by a distinguished steering group, whose members generously shared their expertise: Ann Keane, Her Majesty's Chief Inspector of Education and Training in Wales; Nigel Vaughan, Secondary Sector Lead Inspector, Estyn; Gareth Pierce, Chief Executive, WJEC; Anna Brychan, Director, NAHT Cymru; Gary Brace, Chief Executive, General Teaching Council for Wales; Professor Gareth Rees, School of Social Sciences, Cardiff University; Professor David Egan, UWIC; Dr Chris Llewelyn, Deputy Chief Executive, WLGA; and John Osmond, Director, IWA.

We are deeply grateful also to the staff and pupils of Cwmtawe Community School, Newtown High School, St Joseph's R.C. High School, Newport, Ysgol David Hughes and Ysgol y Preseli.

Sir Adrian Webb
Chair of the Steering Group

Executive Summary

Background to the research

The research underlying *Making a difference at Key Stage 3* was conducted in response to observation of an apparent dip in performance among Welsh schoolchildren during Key Stage 3. This dip has persisted over at least a decade. Comparative data suggest that performance in Wales is also falling behind that in other nations. Since Key Stage 3 performance lays the foundations for achievement at Key Stage 4, any indication that results are not as good as they could be is of serious concern.

The purpose of the research was to better understand, within the Welsh context, good practice at Key Stage 3. Having determined the key characteristics of successful schools, we sought to identify commonalities in their implementation. In addition to contributing to our understanding of how successful schools operate, our findings have a number of implications for Welsh education policy.

The first aim of the research was to identify the factors that contribute to outstanding performance. Analysis of data showing the value added by schools between KS2 and KS3 was used to select thirty Welsh secondary schools for further study. These schools were drawn from across the value added spectrum, with an equal number performing better than would be expected, as expected and less well than expected. Cross-referencing of details from their Estyn inspection reports led to identification of eleven factors of particular importance.

To understand which of these factors carries the greatest weight in successful schools, and how they are put into practice in different school environments, a final selection of five schools was made. These schools were shown to be effective by their value added data, examination results and Estyn inspections. Collectively they do not form a representative sample of Welsh schools. They have been chosen for the insight that they can provide into the varied approaches to school improvement taken by successful schools facing quite different circumstances.

Interview-based research, supplemented by documentary evidence, forms the basis for case study reports on each of the schools. In each case the features that contribute to the school's success are identified, and the context within which those features are operationalised is detailed.

The detailed case studies demonstrate that excellent practice is occurring within Wales. There are features of this practice which are common to many or all of the schools. These form the core of their success. It is in the detail of their implementation that the schools vary. This report provides both comprehensive descriptions and a synthesis of the schools' approaches. Taken together, it is hoped that they will inspire and inform practitioners in other schools and local authorities. Although research commenced prior to the release of the 2009 PISA statistics and the subsequent Welsh policy response, the findings also provide insight into five issues addressed in the Education Minister's twenty proposed action points.

Characteristics of successful schools

The case studies revealed five characteristics common to the schools' success at Key Stage 3. Whilst the detail of their implementation varied considerably between schools, a number of commonalities were identified.

Leadership, self-evaluation and external support

— A single, explicit, unifying principle is driven from the top but shared by all.
— Regular, in-depth, honest evaluations are undertaken.
— Evaluations lead to planned actions within set timeframes.
— Staff are held accountable for missed targets.
— The tone of evaluations is positive and supportive.
— Resources are used to free staff to observe good practice within the school and also to seek it elsewhere.
— Formal mechanisms exist for discussing and disseminating good practice.

Ethos

— Pupils' views are sought on academic issues.
— Pupils receive feedback on the actions taken as a result of their input.
— Reward mechanisms, recognising good effort and behaviour, are

applied on a termly or half-termly basis.
— An ethos of respect and care for others is explicitly reinforced still more regularly, through buddying schemes, assemblies and extra-curricular activities.
— Staff are being encouraged to adopt a particularly positive attitude towards pupils who are working to improve their basic skills levels.

Innovation in teaching and learning

— The myriad teaching methods and great creativity employed by teachers are a major strength.
— Teachers have introduced more interactive practices into the classroom.
— Pupils prefer to understand the context for their learning, and to understand what is required of them to progress. Use of Assessment for Learning techniques and closer departmental links help to make these connections.
— Collapsing of timetables for whole-school 'skills days' is a common response to the skills-based curriculum.
— Schools are using key skills accreditation at Level 2 to motivate KS3 pupils of all abilities.

Data gathering and use

— Schools focus on the trajectory of pupils as much as on absolute standards of attainment.
— They maintain all-encompassing databases of pupil information.
— Pupil targets are informed by this wealth of information and incorporate an element of challenge. They are often set, and always monitored, by senior management.
— Targets, and progress against them, are regularly discussed with all pupils.
— A school-wide approach towards assessment is adopted.
— Assessments are a regular part of the school calendar.

Addressing underachievement and basic skills deficits

— The depth of data available on each pupil helps to ensure an appropriately targeted response to underachievement.

- Mentoring of all pupils plays an important consolidatory role, helping pupils to synthesise the information given to them by their subject teachers, reinforcing a message of success and ensuring that pupils are working consistently and effectively.
- Schools adopt an adaptable approach to addressing underachievement that can be tailored to a given intake or individual pupil.
- Only those pupils with the most severe skills deficits are withdrawn from lessons.
- Good use is made of registration periods and PSE lessons to work on literacy, numeracy and key skills with all pupils.
- Learning support assistants have taken on greater responsibility for improving pupils' basic skills.
- Cross-curricular literacy and numeracy initiatives are being adopted.

To achieve the level of success apparent in the case study schools, each factor has required substantial time and energy to be spent on it. That there is no one-off solution to bringing about success is understood by all of the schools. Ongoing commitment to continuous improvement is necessary, and there can therefore be no let-up in the intensity of activity devoted to it.

Central to the schools' success is their ability to balance structure with adaptability. At the same time as having built an approach that encompasses these core factors, all acknowledge an ongoing need for innovation.

Policy implications

The case studies collectively provide insight into five issues addressed in the Education Minister's twenty proposed action points. These are: the decision to pursue a top twenty position in the 2015 PISA tests; the focus on monitoring and evaluation structures; the direction of continuing professional development; the planned implementation of annual pupil- and school-level targets; and increased attention to literacy and numeracy.

Improving performance in PISA

The GCSE examination is predominantly a test of pupils' ability to acquire knowledge. By contrast, the purpose of the OECD's Programme for International Student Assessment (PISA) tests is to measure the extent to which pupils will be able to bring existing and new knowledge to bear in their adult lives. The former assesses acquisition of knowledge, the latter its application. In each case, therefore, the skill-sets required for success are somewhat different.

If pursuit of excellence in both is to be an explicit goal in Wales, careful consideration will need to be given to the creation of a consistent approach to teaching of the relevant knowledge. Yet we must not seek to become accomplished in the PISA tests solely because we have previously failed to achieve highly in them. We must do so only if we believe PISA to be assessing something valuable.

We have not yet seen significant public debate on the fundamental strategic direction of our education system. The question of what ends we desire from the education of our young people must be settled as a matter of urgency. Only from such a strategic sense of purpose can a truly coherent and consistent system of education be formulated.

Monitoring and evaluation

In each of the case study schools rigorous and honest assessment of standards is undertaken. Staff acknowledge that without it neither individual pupils nor the school as a whole would be able to progress.

Nevertheless, and despite past failures to rigorously monitor performance by some schools and at the system level, this does not justify the introduction of an overly prescriptive approach. To demand that all schools follow a process for monitoring and evaluating performance, and for implementing changes in light of that evaluation, is vital for improvement. To prescribe precisely what that process should look like and how it should operate would be as damaging as to continue with a laissez faire approach.

Any national stipulations regarding schools' evaluation frameworks must be flexible enough to permit a diversity of approaches. If schools are to be required to share a rigid adherence to a set of monitoring protocols, the detail of how the protocols are implemented should be allowed to reflect local circumstances.

Continuing professional development

Whilst there is a role for centrally-determined priorities, local context must be allowed to dictate at least part of the content of continuing professional development. Teachers at different stages in their careers, with their own professional interests and working in environments with very particular challenges, will desire and need quite different forms of professional development.

The Welsh Government needs to make sure that there is a supply of high quality graduates for teaching and senior management posts. It also needs to guarantee funding to allow teachers to undertake continuing professional development and observe good practice elsewhere in the system. This will ensure that schools have the capacity to undertake rigorous evaluations and to plan and implement new strategies.

Judicious use of targets

Targets have a part to play in any monitoring process, but they provide only a narrow indicator of success. If targets are the only means by which schools' trajectory and absolute standard are judged, the rational response will be to alter behaviour to meet them. There is, however, no guarantee that a response to these short term demands will be in the best interests of a school and its pupils in the longer term. To avoid short term gaming behaviour, targets should be used with extreme caution.

However carefully chosen the targets, a school's success cannot be reduced to performance against them. The case study schools' own monitoring procedures show just how complex and demanding a process it is to maintain an upward trajectory. The government must therefore consider how local authorities can be best equipped to develop detailed knowledge of the subtleties of their schools' performance and to engage in in-depth partnerships to support them.

Focusing on literacy and numeracy

The government's planned focus on literacy and numeracy mirrors efforts in the case study schools to ensure that all pupils have the skills necessary to access the curriculum.

The schools' unrelenting commitment to identifying and tackling poor literacy and numeracy represents, however, only one part of their efforts to achieve the best outcomes for every pupil. A nuanced understanding of individual needs, flexibility of approach and creativity all make a significant contribution to the successful engagement of pupils.

Development of pupils' literacy and numeracy skills is critical, but must not be pursued at the expense of teachers' freedom to motivate and challenge their pupils. A balance must therefore be struck. A structured response to low literacy and numeracy levels must still allow schools the flexibility to simultaneously address other causes of underachievement.

Summation

Two forms of monitoring can be identified in relation to school performance. The first is the measurement of outcomes at the system level. The second is the monitoring of progression at the level of the individual pupil or school. This research has identified two distinct policy responses that will be required in relation to these different forms.

In terms of outcomes, the Welsh Government must decide what it desires from our education system, and hence what outputs will be measured. At present we are, effectively by default, measuring performance using two quite different indicators, the GCSE and the PISA test. The choice that exists is whether to set the greatest store by GCSEs, by a combination of GCSE and PISA results, or by a new qualification that embodies the PISA philosophy. This is a difficult and grave decision. Whilst it absolutely must not be taken lightly, it will be necessary for the development of a consistent and effective education system.

The second form of monitoring, of progression, should ideally occur at the school level. Our case studies show that some schools are already operating to a sufficiently high standard to justify being given autonomy. However, the PISA results indicate that this level of autonomy is not yet justified for all schools. This does not mean that those schools should be required to renounce all control over the monitoring of school and pupil progression. The emphasis must be on building internal capacity, to enable ongoing development and allow them to earn autonomy in the medium to long term.

Section 1:

What makes a successful school?

Chapter 1:
Project background and rationale

The major policy challenge of raising attainment in Welsh secondary schools, particularly at Key Stage (KS) 3, has persisted throughout the past decade. In 2011 it has taken on a new urgency. An identified need for improvements in attainment has tended to be predicated on comparisons of pupil performance at age 11 (end of Key Stage 2) with that at age 14 (end of Key Stage 3). The nature of the challenge so described is starkly illustrated in Table 1. These figures are by no means anomalous, this dip in performance at KS3 when compared with KS2 attainment being evident at least as early as 2000 and having remained relatively consistent since.

Table 1: *Percentage of 2009 Welsh Key Stage 3 cohort attaining the expected level, by teacher assessment, at Key Stages 2 and 3*[1].

	English	Mathematics	Science
Key Stage 2 (2006)	79	81	86
Key Stage 3 (2009)	69	72	74

This study takes as its starting point the apparent existence of a 'Key Stage 3 dip' within Wales. However, whilst national and international comparisons are not the focus of this work, it must also be acknowledged that its publication comes at a time of just such comparisons. The December 2010 release of the latest internationally standardised PISA test results has incited vigorous debate about the current state and future direction of the Welsh education system. The 2009 results show Welsh fifteen year olds not only to be falling behind their counterparts in England, Scotland and Northern Ireland,

---

1   Welsh Assembly Government, 2010, 'Assessment and Examination Performance in Wales: Comparison with England and its Regions, 2009', Statistical Bulletin SB 47/2010.

but also to be performing below the OECD average, as Table 2 shows.

Table 2: *Performance in the OECD Programme for International Student Assessment (PISA) tests in reading, mathematics and science, 2009 and 2006[2].*

| | Points scores | | | | | |
| | Reading | | Mathematics | | Science | |
	2009	2006	2009	2006	2009	2006
Wales	476	481	472	484	496	505
England	495	496	493	495	515	516
Northern Ireland	499	495	492	494	511	508
Scotland	500	499	499	506	514	515
OECD average	493	492	496	498	501	500

The case can of course be made that the figures are not directly comparable and that there is therefore too high a degree of uncertainty to be able to pass judgement. However, since KS3 performance lays the foundations for achievement at KS4, any indication that results are not as good as they could be is of serious concern.

In 2008, only 58% of Welsh pupils reached the Level 2 threshold, of five A*-C passes at GCSE or equivalent, a figure which fell to 45.6% with the additional requirement of A*-C passes in English or Welsh and mathematics. In England these figures were 64.8% and 47.3% respectively. In the same year, over thirteen percent of pupils in Wales failed to reach the Level 1 threshold (five passes at A*-G)[3]. The implications for these individuals' life chances are stark. One in four of the Welsh working age population is functionally illiterate and one in six has no qualifications[4]. Twelve percent of

---

2   OECD, 2010, 'PISA 2009 results: Volume I, What students know and can do: student performance in reading, mathematics and science' and OECD, 2007, 'PISA 2006 Volume 2: Data', www.pisa.oecd.org

3   Welsh Assembly Government, 2009, 'Assessment and Examination Performance in Wales: Comparison with England and its Regions, 2008', Statistical Bulletin SB 36/2009.

4   Equality and Human Rights Commission, 2010, 'How fair is Britain? Equality, human rights and good relations in 2010. The first triennial review.'

16-18 year olds and 21.6% of 19-24 year olds in Wales are currently not in education, employment or training[5].

Although the proportion of pupils achieving the expected level at KS3 has risen steadily over the past decade, a further concern in Wales is that the gap between the best and worst performing schools remains broadly constant[6]. This gap has been shown to be greater at KS3 than at any other Key Stage[7]. However, the existence of schools which successfully overcome challenging circumstances suggests that it should be possible to implement interventions that will improve consistency and narrow this gap.

From these observations, three questions of particular interest emerge:

— What factors, both at a whole-school level and in relation to Key Stage 3, contribute to outstanding performance?
— How are these factors put into practice in different school environments?
— What lessons can be learnt from these findings by schools and by policy makers?

In addressing these questions, the research that underlies this report comprised three phases:

Phase I
Ranking and cross-referencing of all Welsh maintained schools according to KS2-KS3 Model 2a Contextual Value Added data for the three years 2006-2008.

Contextual value added data control for effects other than school effect on pupil performance. This allows the impact on performance of the school to be more accurately identified.

Using these data in combination with information on the date of each school's most recent Estyn inspection, from an initial list of 222 secondary schools thirty were chosen for further analysis in Phase II. These consisted of ten schools that have displayed significant positive added value in at least

---

5   See www.statswales.gov.uk, Post 16 Education and Training, Key Education Statistics,
         Proportion of young people not in education, employment or training, 2009 figures.

6   Estyn's Annual Report 2009-2010 states that 'the proportion of secondary schools with
         good or better standards has generally stayed the same', whilst 'the proportion having
         important shortcomings ... is similar to that which existed six years ago'.

7   National Assembly for Wales, 2002, 'Narrowing the Gap in the Performance of Schools'.

two of the three study years, ten that had KS3 outcomes not significantly different from those predicted, and ten that have produced results which are significantly worse than expected.

Phase II
Creation of a preliminary list of characteristics that constitute outstanding performance and contribute to added value at KS3.

Analysis of the thirty schools' most recent Estyn reports was undertaken. The reports were mined for evidence of factors contributing to high or low value added. Some of these factors are specific to KS3 and others impact at the whole-school level. Particular attention was paid to finding detailed descriptions of how good practice is operationalised in schools, in order to inform the questioning employed in Phase III.

Context for these findings was provided by reference to a range of academic and policy documents on school effectiveness. The preliminary findings of Phase II were also presented at the IWA's Learning Pathways conference in February 2010, so as to solicit the opinions of other experts in the field.

Phase III
Case study investigation of how outstanding features are put into practice within different school environments.

From the thirty schools studied in Phase II, five were selected for more detailed investigation. These schools demonstrated outstanding performance in one or more of the areas identified in Phase II. Semi-structured interviews were conducted with staff and students.

Recognising the limited utility of decontextualised lists of outstanding features, the end purpose of Phase III was to contextualise these features, giving a more detailed description of their implementation and the conditions under which they produce a positive effect.

A description of the project method is appended to this report. Also appended is a full explanation of Phase I, the statistical analysis which underpins the later stages of the research. Phase II, the identification of factors contributing to outstanding performance, and Phase III, the contextualisation of those factors, are discussed in the following chapters.

Chapter 2:
Factors linked to outstanding performance

Previous Welsh studies on school effectiveness have identified a number of factors that contribute to outstanding performance. The Assembly's 'Narrowing the Gap' report[7], for instance, identified three factors that are key to improving school performance in deprived areas. These are having key personnel in a position to drive improvement, monitoring teaching and promoting effective practice, and making effective use of attainment data. A further four areas of focus, namely KS2 to KS3 transition, literacy skills, behaviour management and attendance, were also deemed important.

More recently, Estyn's report on tackling disadvantage in schools[8] noted the outcomes of the Government's programme to 'Raise Attainment and Individual Standards in Education' (RAISE) in relation to school effectiveness. A shared vision, including through partnership with parents and the community, effective monitoring practices, and the development of pupils' social and emotional skills were all considered critical. In addition, schools in deprived areas were considered to benefit particularly from highly effective leadership, consistently good teaching, provision of extra-curricular and out-of-hours activities, high expectations of both standards and behaviour and a willingness to develop the curriculum according to pupils' needs.

In addition to these factors, Estyn reported the effectiveness of increasing the expertise of teaching assistants. Schools that are successful in this regard have engaged assistants in analysing performance data and delivering specific strategies to enhance key skills. Estyn also foregrounded the role of the local authority. This is an element of the partnership approach not highlighted in individual school inspection reports, but nevertheless constitutes an important part of the context for school success. Elements of local authority intervention previously described by schools in Wales as

---

8   Estyn, 2010, 'Tackling child poverty and disadvantage in schools'. See also Estyn, 2009, 'The impact of RAISE 2008-2009'.

being particularly effective include support for literacy and numeracy initiatives and for the application of pupil performance data to identification of necessary improvements[9].

These studies can be situated within the context of a broad academic literature on school effectiveness[10]. The factors identified as most significant and the terminology used have by no means been agreed upon[11], but reviews of the literature have identified a number of common characteristics. Sammons et al.'s 1995 typology consists of eleven key factors[12]:

— Professional leadership – including a clear sense of purpose and devolved management responsibility stemming from the headteacher's leading role.

— Shared vision and goals – comprising unity of purpose, consistency of practice and collaboration.

— A learning environment – creation of a positive climate for learning.

— Concentration on learning and teaching – maximising learning time, learning opportunities and academic achievement.

— Purposeful teaching – teaching is efficient and structured, has a clear purpose and is adaptive.

— High expectations – high expectations and intellectual challenge are universal and are communicated to all.

9   Audit Commission, Local Government Summary, January 2008, 'National school survey results 2007. Schools' views of their council's services and the services provided locally for children and young people (Wales)'.

10   A wealth of publications on school effectiveness is available on the High Reliability Schools website, www.highreliabilityschools.com/Shared/SchoolEffectiveness.aspx

11   B. Witziers and R. Bosker, 1997, 'A meta-analysis on the effects of presumed school effectiveness enhancing factors', available at www.highreliabilityschools.com

12   P. Sammons, J. Hillman and P. Mortimore, 1995, 'Key characteristics of effective schools: A review of school effectiveness research'. See also D. Reynolds, 1997, 'School effectiveness: retrospect and prospect', Scottish Educational Review 29(2): 97-113 and T. Wendell, 2000, 'Creating equity and quality', Kelowna: SAEE for references to this and other typologies.

— Positive reinforcement – pupils are subject to clear and fair discipline and are given feedback.

— Monitoring progress – both pupil and school performance are monitored.

— Pupil rights and responsibilities – positive self-esteem is developed through good pupil-staff relationships, and pupils are given positions of responsibility.

— Home-school partnership – parental involvement is encouraged.

— A learning organisation – school-based staff development occurs.

Similar preoccupations, albeit differently worded, are apparent in the content of the School Effectiveness Framework, which is currently being rolled out across Wales. The Framework is designed as a single process for reform across the Welsh school system and consists of six elements: leadership; working with others; networks of professional practice; intervention and support; improvement and accountability; and curriculum and teaching. These are intended to constitute a means of thinking and acting systematically for the improvement of Welsh education, and will be applied at the national, local and individual learner level[13].

The factors set out above are those considered to contribute to effective practice at the whole-school level. However, given the focus of this research, as outlined above, it was deemed necessary to identify those effectiveness factors with a particular relevance at Key Stage 3 and in a Welsh context. This was achieved through reference to a sample of recent Estyn inspection reports.

Reports were obtained for the thirty schools identified through statistical analysis (Appendix 2). With particular reference to the factors outlined above, these were mined for information on elements of practice at KS3 that were considered either outstanding or in need of development. Particular attention was paid to finding detail on how factors that contribute

---

13   Welsh Assembly Government, 2008, 'School Effectiveness Framework. Building effective learning communities together'.

to good practice are operationalised. This led to the identification of eleven consistently important factors. Each factor comprises a number of distinct but related features:

Leadership

— Strong sense of vision and direction, shared by all
— Appropriate delegation from headteacher to SMT, middle management and departments
— Strong role of governors as 'critical friends'
— Good communication
— Time reserved for managers to effectively carry out roles

Teaching

— Tailoring work to individual needs
— Structured and well planned lessons with clear objectives
— High expectations of performance
— Challenge and pace
— Engagement of pupils in their own learning
— Teacher enthusiasm
— Well qualified teachers who are able regularly to update their skills/knowledge
— Varied teaching methods, including use of independent working

Broad and flexible curriculum, incorporating key skills provision across subjects

Effective Special Educational Needs (SEN) provision

Assessment

— Rigorous
— Detailed
— Clear identification of how pupils can improve

Monitoring and targets

— Effective use of data to set targets for school improvement
— Understanding individual pupil needs to set personalised targets
— Consistency of monitoring and application of plans across whole school
— Sharing of good practice
— Use of self evaluation and school development plan to link policy to practice
— Realistic approach to target setting

Attendance

— Consistently high attendance by pupils and staff
— Punctuality
— Limiting and managing exclusions

Behaviour

— High expectations
— Positive relationships with teachers
— Support for those with behavioural difficulties
— Pupils given voice, as for example through the School Council

Care and guidance

— Promotion of moral/social/spiritual/cultural values
— Tackling disaffection

Partnerships

— With parents, including detailed reporting of pupil progress
— With primary schools, including curricular and pastoral links
— With local communities, to establish shared values

Extra-curricular activities and out-of-hours learning opportunities

Chapter 3:
Overview of schools selected for in-depth study

Analysis of the Estyn reports for the thirty schools selected for Phase II fulfilled a dual purpose. Firstly, it provided an initial list of factors contributing to outstanding performance, for use in the Phase III interviews. Secondly, it served to highlight those schools with the most to offer to that final phase.

Following completion of the first two research phases, discussions were held with the Secondary Sector Lead Inspector at Estyn. This led to the selection of six schools for study in the third phase of the research. Of these six, one withdrew from the study at a sufficiently late stage to prevent its replacement. As discussion of the remaining five schools shows, this has not impacted on the range of attributes displayed in the case study schools and therefore does not significantly limit our ability to draw conclusions with a relevance beyond these institutions.

Interviews were conducted with key staff, including members of the senior management team, teachers from a variety of subjects, learning support assistants, and other staff with responsibility for basic skills development and transition arrangements. Students from each school were also interviewed. A draft report on each school was prepared using evidence from these interviews, following which the senior management teams from each school were invited to engage in a dialogue about possible amendments and additions. It is worth noting that, although alterations were made in response to schools' comments, no major discrepancies were found between the outcome of the interviews and managers' own interpretations of each school's approach. Indeed, several headteachers made a point of noting that the reports succeeded in capturing the essence of their schools.

The five schools in which detailed research took place are:

— Cwmtawe Community School, Neath Port Talbot (1)
— Newtown High School, Powys (2)
— St Joseph's R.C. High School, Newport (3)

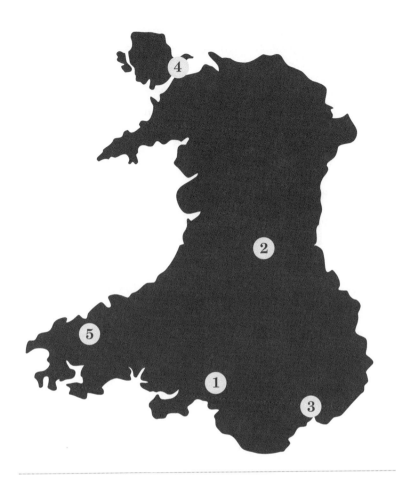

— Ysgol David Hughes, Anglesey (4)
— Ysgol y Preseli, Pembrokeshire (5)

The rationale for selecting each of the schools is set out below.

Overview
The five schools identified for further study in Phase III have not been selected with the intention of providing a representative sample of all secondary schools in Wales. Given the research project's stated aim of exploring how the factors that contribute to excellent performance at KS3 are put into practice, the selected schools show a deliberate skew towards

good or excellent performance. This notwithstanding, the chosen schools represent a broad cross-section when compared on a range of attributes.

Based on the free school meal indicator[14], three schools have below average deprivation, one has deprivation approximating to the national average and one has an above average concentration of pupils from deprived backgrounds.

Three schools demonstrated consistently high value added at Key Stage 3 across the study period, 2006-2008. One of these schools was judged in 2003 to have 'serious weaknesses', and has therefore undergone a period of significant and rapid improvement. A further two schools had, according to the KS2-KS3 CVA measure, KS3 results during this period that were no higher or lower than would be expected given pupil intake; however, both schools produce absolute KS3 results that surpass local and national averages, and also produce GCSE results that are well above average[15].

In terms of geographical location, one school is in north-west Wales, one is in mid Wales, one is in south-west Wales, one is in a south Wales valleys community and one is located in the coastal urban belt of south-east Wales. Two schools serve predominantly urban areas, and three serve rural or semi-rural catchments.

The sample includes one faith school (St Joseph's) and two naturally bilingual schools (Ysgol y Preseli and Ysgol David Hughes).

Thus although representing too small a sample, and therefore not intended, to be fully representative of the Welsh secondary sector, these schools nevertheless illustrate the varied characteristics of secondary schools in Wales. They also display a wide geographical spread. At the same time, they collectively meet the requirements of the study for a split between schools that are sustaining good performance at KS3, those that are in the process of, or have recently undergone, a period of improvement, and those that

---

14   www.statswales.wales.gov.uk, Schools and Teachers, Schools Census – School Level, Schools Census 2010, Free School Meals, 'Pupils eligible for free school meals 2010 – Secondary schools'. National average FSM eligibility for 2009/10 was 15.6%.

15   It is worth noting that 'traditionally high achieving schools may be limited in their potential to achieve a high value added score'. See Welsh Assembly Government, 2009, 'Key Stage 3 and 4 Value Added Notes for Guidance' (Statistical Reference Bulletin) for an explanation.

perform broadly as expected at KS3 but nevertheless show evidence of excellent practice.

Cwmtawe Community School

At the time of its last inspection, in 2006, Cwmtawe Community School was rated as 'good with outstanding features' in six of the seven key questions. Although Phase I identified it as not having added significant value at KS3 between 2006 and 2008, it is notable for its consistently high results at KS4.

The school is within Neath Port Talbot LEA, which was identified in Estyn's 2010 report on tackling child poverty and disadvantage as a local authority area in which disadvantaged pupils achieve well at secondary level.

Cwmtawe is a large 11-16 co-educational school, with over 1200 pupils on its roll, and has a wide catchment area encompassing large parts of the Swansea Valley. At present 17% of pupils are entitled to free school meals[14]; although this is not very far above the national average, Estyn identifies 'a large proportion of the [catchment] area [as being] economically and socially disadvantaged'.

The majority of pupils are first-language English speakers. Approximately 7% speak Welsh as a first language and 4% are from minority ethnic backgrounds. Literacy skills are significantly lower than LEA and national averages at intake.

Newtown High School

Last inspected in 2008, Newtown High School, an 11-18 comprehensive in Powys, received a positive report, having previously been judged to have serious weaknesses. According to Estyn, the 'improvement in standards and provision ... is outstanding'.

The data analysed in Phase I of this study, for the years 2006-2008, show that KS3 results were subject to significant value added in three consecutive years. This confirms the assessment of the Secondary Sector Lead Inspector that this is a rapidly improving and high performing school.

Based on 2010 figures, free school meal uptake is, at 15.9%, at approximately the national average[14], although Estyn judge there to be a 'significant minority of pupils' from homes in relative economic and social disadvantage. There are just over 800 pupils on the roll, drawn from both the town of Newtown and its rural surroundings.

St Joseph's R.C. High School

St Joseph's R.C. High School is an 11-18 Catholic faith school within the city of Newport. It added significant value at KS3 in two of the three years 2006-2008, and also performs well at KS4.

The school prioritises admission of children from the Catholic faith, who comprise 70% of the 1400 pupils on the school roll. The remaining 30% of pupils are drawn from other Christian denominations and faiths. As a faith school, St Joseph's attracts pupils from across the region, although the majority are from Newport itself.

11.7% of pupils are entitled to free school meals[14], a level below the national average. Pupils come from a range of socio-economic backgrounds. Approximately 5% of pupils speak English as an additional language, none of whom were first-language Welsh speakers at the time of the school's last inspection in 2007.

Ysgol David Hughes

Ysgol David Hughes, Anglesey, is a bilingual 11-18 comprehensive school with approximately 1100 pupils on the roll. Of the eight forms in Year 7, three study 70% of the curriculum through the medium of Welsh, three receive an equal amount of teaching in English and Welsh, and two forms are taught for 70% of their time in English.

Although identified in Phase I of this research as adding no statistically significant value in the years 2006-2008, Ysgol David Hughes is described in its most recent Estyn inspection as 'a very good school with many outstanding features'.

Ysgol David Hughes serves the south-east of the Isle of Anglesey. In the school's catchment area agriculture predominates, with some light industry. Deprivation – as proxied by free school meal uptake – is low, at 8.9%[14], but has been rising in recent years.

Ysgol y Preseli
Ysgol y Preseli is a bilingual 11-18 co-educational secondary school in rural Pembrokeshire. Both its latest inspection report, from 2008, and its added value results – which had a statistically significant positive value in two of the three years for which data were studied – confirm it to be a consistently high performing school at KS3.

Of approximately 950 pupils on the school roll, 65% come from homes with English as the first language. 35% come from predominantly Welsh-speaking homes, a proportion that is currently diminishing.

Only 6.4% of pupils are entitled to free school meals[14], although Estyn reports that 75% of the school population is drawn from areas of economic disadvantage in which household income is below the national average. The school catchment area includes the towns of Haverfordwest, Pembroke and Fishguard, from where one quarter of pupils are drawn.

Note on the case study chapters
The case study chapters provide a detailed description of activity in each of a number of key areas at Key Stage 3. During the interview phase, the questions posed referred to the eleven factors identified in Phase II of the research. However, the importance that respondents attributed to each factor – and the way in which they are put into practice within schools – was by no means the same in every case. Each school is achieving or working towards the highest standards at Key Stage 3 through a unique application of the factors.

Although commonalities are apparent between the schools – as reflected in similarities in the structure of each chapter – the case studies have been structured to highlight features of particular interest in relation to each school's practice at Key Stage 3. The chapters should therefore not be read as direct comparisons of the schools.

Chapter 4:
Characteristics of successful schools

Each of the case study schools draws together a large number of practices in its pursuit of success, and the extent to which each factor figures as a significant feature in this process is highly context dependent.

This notwithstanding, five factors are of particular note. These are features which are apparent in all, or almost all, of the case study schools and which show a degree of consistency in the way in which they are put into practice.

They are:
— leadership, self-evaluation and the use of external support;
— ethos, encompassing pupil engagement and the motivation and challenge of pupils;
— innovation in teaching and learning;
— the gathering and use of data; and
— approaches to resolving underachievement and basic skills deficits.

What unites all five of these factors is the dedication of staff to their implementation, the rigorous standards applied to the selected strategies, and the depth with which those strategies are implemented.

To achieve the level of success apparent in these schools, each factor has required substantial time and energy to be spent on it. That there is no one-off solution to bringing about success is understood by all of the schools. Ongoing commitment to continuous improvement is necessary, and there can therefore be no let-up in the intensity of activity devoted to it.

In an environment that places pupil development at its core, and in the context of shared responsibility and openness to new practices, underpinned by clear accountability structures, this is a professional challenge that teaching staff and managers have shown themselves to be willing to meet.

Leadership, self-evaluation and external support

Each of the schools has a headteacher whose vision for the school permeates down through the school, from staff to students. Only some of these schools encapsulate that vision in a prominent word or phrase – such as Newtown's 'CYFLE' or Preseli's motto of 'remember to learn how to live' – but in all cases it is understood in terms of commitment to the moral purpose of achieving the best for, and from, every pupil.

This explicit, unifying principle is driven from the top, but must be shared by all to be effective. In each of the schools strong leadership from the headteacher is balanced by a high level of trust in others' abilities, and by an associated devolution of responsibility to senior and middle managers. This enables the schools to bring to bear the strengths of multiple individuals. It also creates the capacity to trial new initiatives in parts of the school before their wholesale adoption. In terms of professional fulfilment, it is evident that staff value highly the opportunities that this devolution of responsibility affords them.

The evidence suggests that, to be effective, this approach must be underpinned by clear lines of accountability and rigorous monitoring and evaluation procedures. Effective monitoring and self-evaluation should highlight, at an early stage, issues requiring improvement. Detailed action plans must then be formulated to address these issues. These processes provide the evidence that allows senior managers to build and sustain faith in the innovation and experimentation undertaken by teachers.

Rigorous self-evaluation

The self-evaluation process at Newtown High School was variously described by staff as 'rigorous', 'very thorough' and 'incredibly useful'. Even staff who have experience of innovative procedures in other schools are impressed by the thoroughness of self-evaluation at Newtown. The headteacher has distilled the Estyn inspection criteria into a grid that forms the basis for an annual evaluation. This feeds, in turn, into faculty and departmental improvement plans.

Regular meetings are held between heads of department and their link managers at which self-evaluation reports, improvement plans and examination results are discussed. Although staff are 'not let off' if targets are not met, they are 'valued as professionals, for our professional judgement' and given all necessary support. Teachers regard this positive and supportive approach to self-evaluation as vitally important ∎

Specific methods of evaluation, be they self-evaluations based on Estyn's inspection criteria or lesson observation by senior management, vary between the schools. Nevertheless, all display common features in their execution and outcomes:

— Evaluations are regular, in-depth and honest.

— They lead to planned actions within set timeframes. These feed back into the monitoring process in an iterative process of improvement.

— Where targets are not met, staff are held accountable and required to make provisions for future improvements.

— This notwithstanding, the tone of evaluations is positive. Teaching staff and management engage in a dialogue and work to achieve consensus on a way forward.

Video evidence of successful lessons

Ysgol y Preseli is planning to video good practice in the classroom. Members of the school's professional learning community will use the videos to start discussions among staff about lesson structure and delivery. As a senior manager notes, 'it's quite easy to say that for an exceptional lesson we want to see this, this, this and this. But when you see it in practice, you get a better idea of what makes an exceptional lesson' ∎

Accountability structures provide the framework within which new ideas can be carefully tested, but the schools are also characterised by a culture of openness to seeking out and implementing the best new approaches.

Resources are used to free staff to observe other lessons and to visit other schools in which elements of innovative or best practice are evident. All of the schools have in place formal mechanisms for dissemination and discussion of good practice, from twilight meetings and learning fora to professional learning communities. Awareness of best practice requires senior management and heads of department to monitor practice not only internally but across the sector.

In the latter regard the role of local authority advisors can be paramount. As an Anglesey school, Ysgol David Hughes has access to the Cynnal advisory service. Operating outside the day-to-day demands of the teaching environment, Cynnal advisors can devote time to finding and presenting examples of good practice, and relating these to policy requirements. In Pembrokeshire, Ysgol y Preseli has benefited from the authority-wide Effective Learning Group: in addition to benefiting from access to external expertise, schools can save resources by sharing the findings of staff who have attended conferences and seminars.

Engaging with external advisors

Staff in all departments at Ysgol David Hughes use the local authority advisory service Cynnal to support their work. The Cynnal science advisor, for instance, has been working with every catchment area in Anglesey and Gwynedd to develop a more consistent understanding of levels between all primary and secondary schools. Meanwhile literacy skills are being targeted through the development of grammar guidelines for all departments. The advisors provide 'a lot of input' which, because it comes from outside Ysgol David Hughes, increases confidence that the school is up to date with current thinking ∎

Sharing good practice

St Joseph's R.C. High School has recently developed a series of professional learning communities within the school to identify and share good practice. These build on the successes of the pre-existing school Learning Forum. The after-school Forum provides teachers with a platform to discuss new developments that they have implemented. It was as a result of one such meeting that Philosophy for Children was rolled out across the school from its starting point in the English department ■

Ethos

Staff from across the case study schools were at pains to point out that their school is run for the benefit of the pupils – that it is, in effect, the pupils' school. This has important implications both for pupil voice and for the ethos of the school.

The importance of understanding and responding to pupils' opinions on their own learning is increasingly being recognised. School Councils are accordingly gaining in status. All of the schools are moving away from a narrow focus on pastoral matters to also engage their pupils in discussions about pedagogic issues. In some cases the role played by pupils in academic respects is already highly developed and systematic. In other cases it is a still-developing aspect of school life.

In every case pupils have been asked to discuss *how* they like to learn, and in some cases even *what* they would like to learn. Pupil evaluation of modules is also regarded as an important means of ensuring that they are engaged by, and able to comprehend, lesson content. Pupils reported an increased sense of motivation where they have been thus engaged.

An important element of this engagement is that pupils receive feedback on their comments. This includes feedback from teachers and governors to the School Council, displays on notice boards detailing what changes have been made, and immediately apparent changes to the structure and content of lessons. Feedback serves to confirm to pupils that their views are taken seriously and have an impact.

Giving pupils responsibility

Ysgol y Preseli places a great deal of store by the opinions of its pupils. Pupil engagement with the life of the school is characterised by a high level of trust and expectation, with one of the most telling roles in this regard being the contribution of the School Council to staff appointments. Council members interview candidates individually, before feeding back their opinions to the Board of Governors. Pupils are also encouraged to support each other, both through a formal 'buddy' system and informally, and the degree of care shown for others is a particularly striking aspect of the atmosphere within the school. As one pupil said: 'I know now if I see someone looking sad or looking alone it's a responsibility of mine to go and see if this person's alright.' Another described Ysgol y Preseli as being 'like a family' and concluded: 'I know it's a cliche, but the whole school is just as one'.

The extent to which pupils are actively engaged in the life of the school has risen, but so too have the expectations placed on them. The use of targets creates a culture of challenge and, alongside this, schools have introduced a range of mechanisms for recognising and rewarding the pupils who rise to this challenge. Although they take a variety of forms, all are regularly applied – usually on a termly or half-termly basis. A focus on effort as opposed to absolute standards of attainment is also characteristic.

An ethos of respect and care for others is similarly espoused and this, too, is regularly reinforced. Pastoral and academic buddying schemes, which pair older pupils with those lower down the school, assemblies and extra-curricular activities can all be seen as means of reinforcing a sense of collegiality and pride in the school. This positive approach serves to instil and maintain enthusiasm and motivation but, where necessary, standards are enforced through sanctions.

Learning to Learn

The Learning to Learn module is taught to all Ysgol David Hughes pupils in the first term of Year 7. This introduces different learning styles and strategies that pupils might need or choose to employ. The deputy headteacher described the aim as being 'to get the message across from the very beginning that pupils *can* learn, they all have the ability to learn, and to try to get them motivated and to understand that, even though they're not all the same in the way that they learn and the speed at which they learn, they all have an ability to make progress and to improve. It's not a competition – they're improving against their own personal targets'.

Creating a culture of high expectations

From a 2003 Estyn inspection that categorised it as having 'serious weaknesses', Newtown High School has been turned around to the point of exhibiting 'outstanding features'. Central to this has been the creation of an ethos that celebrates good behaviour, effort and achievement. Members of the senior management team set challenging targets for each pupil in every subject, and progress is monitored according to the 'NTU' system: pupils can be 'U', under target, 'T', on target, or 'N', working above target at 'Newtown standard'. One pupil described how being on target is only 'satisfactory'.

Every half term the hardest working pupils in each department are awarded faculty achievement, or 'FAB', badges. Termly 'clean slate reward days', during which pupils have an early lunch and watch a film, recognise all pupils who have received no more than two detentions. Staff believe that the combination of aspirational targets, tangible incentives and the rewarding of pupils from across the ability spectrum has helped to make it 'cool to succeed'. ■

Innovation in teaching and learning

Staff in all of the case study schools showed themselves to be open to trialling new approaches to teaching and learning. Myriad teaching methods have been adopted by teachers, and this variety itself can be regarded as a strength. Both pupils and teachers recognised the role of variety in maintaining interest.

Strategies such as small group work and their active engagement in the lesson were specifically mentioned by pupils in positive terms, as was the use of various technologies. The adoption of Philosophy for Children at St Joseph's is just one example of how the schools have moved away from a 'chalk and talk' approach towards far more interactive practices.

Adopting a new philosophy

The principles of Philosophy for Children have been adopted by teachers at St Joseph's R.C. High School. The purpose of Philosophy for Children (P4C) is to encourage pupils to reflect and talk more within lessons, moving the teacher to the role of a facilitator who guides the pupils towards a deeper understanding of themes and concepts. In a P4C lesson, the entire lesson is devoted to a 'community of enquiry', in which pupils think about and discuss a single theme. Typically, St Joseph's pupils will be shown a stimulus, which might include poems, a song or images, that relates to the theme under discussion. The pupils then formulate a question about what they have seen and spend the remainder of the lesson answering that question. Improved outcomes have already been observed. Whilst the focus of these lessons is on oracy, staff have noticed that 'if oral communication improves then it tends to be that so does the writing'.∎

Pupils were most in agreement on the fact that it helps if they can see a purpose to their studies: they are more attentive when they understand the wider context. An extension of this is that pupils are helped by an understanding of their current standard and what will be required to progress. To this end there has been a widespread introduction of Assessment for Learning principles. The wider contextualisation of individual subjects has been much aided by the introduction in 2008 of the skills-based curriculum. Teachers reported their increased engagement with colleagues in other departments as they seek to introduce consistency through the themes taught and the skills employed.

A recurring statement was that the schools were largely 'traditional' in their continued teaching of pupils by subject. All, however, had found their own responses to the skills-based curriculum. The temporary collapsing of timetables, for several days at a time, was the most common school-wide response. Widely enjoyed by pupils, and valued for their contextualisation of subject content, skills days cover many of the six key skills[16] at one time. Teachers' engagement in these cross-cutting activities has helped to reinforce skills teaching in the classroom. Thus although pupils are still taught in subject-based lessons, the content and style of teaching has altered.

Key skills accreditation is also widespread. Portfolios are by and large

---

16   The six key skills are (1) improving own learning performance, (2) working with others, (3) problem solving, (4) communication, (5) IT and (6) application of number.

completed using work undertaken in subject lessons, although personal and social education (PSE) lessons are also used for the collation of evidence. In one case skills days are explicitly focused on pupils' achievement of accreditation. Accreditation has two main benefits: it provides pupils who have a low chance of achieving sufficient GCSEs to reach the Level 2 threshold with Level 2 qualifications; and it provides a goal for all pupils, including the most able, who without a clear source of motivation might see a levelling off, or even drop, in performance at Key Stage 3.

Skills days

Ysgol David Hughes is one of a number of schools to introduce skills days, during which the ordinary timetable is suspended to make way for a cross-curricular project. Skills days have been implemented in preference to the permanent merging of subjects for the purpose of thematic teaching in the humanities or arts. This latter approach was considered but, following discussions among teaching staff, it was determined that more limited suspension of the timetable is better suited to Ysgol David Hughes' circumstances. The school is working to ensure that all subjects contribute to the skills agenda and is finding that, as more departments become involved in the skills days, teachers are increasingly able to see how pupils work in different settings and are feeding that knowledge back into the classroom ∎

Challenging KS3 pupils to achieve Level 2 qualifications

Recognition that there is significant cross-over between Key Stage 3 courses and the requirements for Level 2 qualifications has led Newtown High School to introduce a range of such qualifications for Year 9 pupils. Staff acknowledge that this will require significant commitment and hard work by teachers and pupils. However, their commitment to 'CYFLE' – both 'opportunity' and the belief that 'caring yields a flourishing learning environment' – means that they believe this to be worthwhile.

The challenge of working towards Level 2 qualifications is intended to provide pupils with a clear goal, thus improving motivation, and to take pupils some way towards achieving the Level 2 threshold, hence relieving pressure at Key Stage 4.

Subjects offered, or planned to be offered, at GCSE level include Welsh, French and humanities. These will be available to the top sets, although the introduction of more modular GCSEs should allow an increasing number of pupils to study at this level. For all pupils, but most particularly for the benefit of those at risk of missing the Level 2 threshold, Newtown has also introduced a range of skills qualifications ▪

In every school, teachers' approach to the content and style of their lessons is marked by a high level of creativity. Whilst some resources – notably on crime scene investigation – are widely used, most arise from individual teachers' imagination and experience and are so diverse as to prevent the identification of any common trends.

What *is* consistent is the thought and effort devoted to creating resources that meet local needs – be that disengaged boys or gifted and talented pupils – and that engage and enthuse.

It is clear that the freedom to take a creative approach is also professionally fulfilling for the teachers. From the creation at Ysgol David Hughes of 'maths mats', which present real life mathematical challenges and tie together content and skills from other subjects, to the filming of DVDs at Cwmtawe for use in transition projects, staff are themselves engaging with and enthused by the learning process. This can only benefit staff morale, which in turn further improves the learning environment.

Data gathering and use
Each of the schools focuses on the trajectory of its pupils as much as on their absolute standard of attainment. Thus all pupils are helped to achieve to the highest standard of which they are capable. To be able to do this most effectively, the schools maintain all-encompassing databases that include records on attendance, behaviour, predicted and actual attainment, effort and additional support needs. These data are gathered from before the pupils arrive in Year 7, through contact with the primary schools, and are regularly updated throughout pupils' time at the school.

The comprehensive datasets held on each pupil have two principal benefits. Firstly, they form the basis for the setting and monitoring of challenging targets. Secondly, having been used to identify pupils who are not reaching those targets, they inform the type of action that is undertaken.

XL@Cwmtawe

Cwmtawe Community School's approach to the gathering and use of data on pupil performance begins when those pupils are still in Year 6. A comprehensive set of data – including information on achievement, attendance, homework completion, support received and behaviour – is requested from feeder primaries.

This informs the single, challenging, target grade given to all pupils in Year 7. It also forms the basis for a monitoring system, known as XL@Cwmtawe, that encompasses effort, achievement and behaviour. A computerised database and ready access to the data from all classrooms allows for the regular sharing of information between subject teachers, form tutors and senior management. This makes possible a rapid and systematic response to pupil underperformance.∎

In four of the five schools targets are set by subject, whilst in one school, Cwmtawe, a single target grade is given to a pupil in Year 7. This latter approach was described as a means of ensuring that pupils' potential is not underestimated in any single subject; pupils are challenged to meet their highest possible potential in every subject.

Although the means of achieving it varies by school, each of the other schools also ensures consistent challenge. In some cases targets are set by the senior management team, but in all cases senior management monitor the progress of year groups and departments, down to the level of the individual pupil. When this is combined with department-level monitoring, it becomes virtually impossible for a pupil to underachieve without somebody becoming aware of it. The depth of data available for that pupil helps to ensure that a response targeted appropriately to the particular causes of his or her underachievement can be designed.

Recognising pupils' capacity

The close relationship between St Joseph's R.C. High School and its partner primaries has led to an improved awareness at St Joseph's of how advanced pupils are by the end of Year 6. The senior management team try to ensure that all NQTs have the opportunity to work with Year 6 pupils, 'so that they see them achieving what they are at the top end of the primary sector, so that we can move them on.' Departments have also altered schemes of work to present greater challenge from the outset, altering the texts offered, revising reading and writing activities and focusing on developing communication skills .

Another common strand in all schools is the discussion of targets, and progress against them, with all pupils. As well as teachers being aware of the areas in which each pupil needs to develop, the pupils are kept informed of, and often encouraged to suggest for themselves, strategies for their personal improvement. Pupils – and their teachers – confirmed that, by understanding what is expected of them and by being actively engaged in their own education, their motivation is increased and they perform better.

A school-wide approach to the assessment and monitoring of performance is shared by all the schools. Performance is gauged on a termly or half-termly basis in all subjects. A variety of assessment techniques is used, from formal examinations to in-class tests. Where formal examinations are timetabled, they create a series of focal points; this is a further source of motivation, since pupils are able to see incremental progress throughout the school year.

All forms of testing provide a snapshot of current performance and rate of progression. Taking *regular* snapshots of performance was consistently described as being critical to the maintenance of pupil progress. Only through regular and comprehensive monitoring can teachers pinpoint the pupils who are at risk of underachieving. Assessing progress across all subjects is also essential, as it serves to emphasise the importance of the target system. Moreover, it contributes to a fuller understanding of a pupil's overall trajectory, and hence to a precise understanding of the causes of underperformance.

Formal examinations

In addition to regular end-of-unit tests, Ysgol y Preseli holds formal examinations twice per year. Senior managers explained that they are used because they focus pupils and provide a 'snapshot' of where they are at present and how they are progressing. Pupils value formal assessment because it 'helps you to understand the level you're at'. It also allows them to feel more prepared for their final examinations: 'you feel like you know what you're doing and you can just get on with it'. The outcomes of these formal tests inform pupils' self-assessment and the school's target-setting processes, so feeding in to efforts to ensure a constant upward trajectory for all pupils throughout their time at Preseli ∎

Clearly monitoring alone is not sufficient to sustain an upward trajectory for all pupils, and the case study schools are united by their use of data to develop strategies for the progression of all.

Addressing underachievement and basic skills deficits

The use of data to identify where support should be targeted begins as soon as pupils arrive in the case study schools. Pupils with the most severe literacy and numeracy skills deficits are immediately subject to intensive programmes aimed at giving them the skills to cope at secondary level.

The nature of the programmes run in each school is varied. Nevertheless, a number of recurring features can be identified. Firstly, the schools tend to withdraw from lessons only the pupils with the most serious needs. Secondly, learning support staff tend to favour giving pupils short bursts of intensive support. In addition to wanting to bring pupils up to a good standard as quickly as possible, they believe that pupils focus far better under such conditions and are more likely to retain what they have learnt. The Catch Up programme sessions favoured by Ysgol David Hughes are, at fifteen minutes per session, a formalised version of a widely favoured strategy.

To some extent limited withdrawal is a consequence of limited resources for addressing basic skills deficits. However, the schools are also intent on ensuring that pupils do not fall further behind in their subject knowledge. They therefore also make full use of the time available to them during registration periods and PSE lessons. In cases where this gives insufficient time to address pupils' needs, schools do consider disapplication of an entire class from a subject or replacement of some subject lessons; these lessons are replaced with basic skills classes.

Because they do not need to be assigned to named pupils during registration periods, learning support assistants are able to provide intensive support during this time. Buddy systems, which pair sixth formers with pupils from lower down the school, are also frequently used. The benefit of using this time to work on literacy and numeracy is that all pupils can be involved, so raising standards across the school.

Tackling poor literacy and numeracy

Cwmtawe Community School has put in place widespread support to address a common cause of underachievement: low levels of literacy and numeracy. Between one third and one half of all pupils receive literacy support at some stage during KS3, and approximately 40-50% of these pupils are in the top band. All pupils work on numeracy skills during one registration period per week. KS3 pupils in the lower bands are also disapplied from French or German in order to receive two basic skills lessons per week. That the headteacher leads a number of these is evidence of the importance attached at the highest level to basic skills development ▪

The role of learning support assistants has evolved in all of the schools. In addition to working with statemented pupils, they also provide more general in-class support in basic skills classes and across the curriculum. Continuing professional development, including NVQ qualification, has allowed many to lead literacy and numeracy programmes and, working to a teacher's lesson plan, to take small numbers of pupils out of class for other targeted support. Some schools are also employing LSAs with specialist knowledge, particularly in the core subjects.

Rising skill levels, specialisation and the increasing autonomy of LSAs mean that the schools are increasing their capacity to support the least able pupils, even as resource constraints challenge that goal. They were agreed, however, that declining resources remain a threat to their ability to achieve the significant improvements that they currently see.

In addition to being highly capable these support assistants care about the children they work with. This was seen as being of paramount importance. Their commitment to the pupils means that, just like the teaching staff, they are willing to put in additional time and effort to ensure a positive outcome.

Developing the role of LSAs

Ysgol y Preseli is one school in which learning support assistants have been given specialised roles. In addition to having LSAs who are assigned to named pupils, the school employs assistants with special expertise in Welsh, English, mathematics and special needs. These assistants work intensively with pupils in the special needs class and with the 'target' group – pupils whose reading age on entry is between nine and eleven years. They are also able to withdraw pupils from registration periods for additional support, making use of all available time to ensure that basic skills deficits are rapidly eliminated. The school aims for only minimal numbers to require ongoing support in Year 8 ∎

Each school has used its own methods for encouraging a positive attitude towards basic skills activities. At Ysgol y Preseli, for instance, staff are encouraged to think of pupils leaving class for literacy support in the same way as they would a pupil leaving for a violin lesson. Up to half of all pupils receiving support at Cwmtawe are in the top band, and support activities have therefore achieved a mainstream status.

The introduction of the skills-based curriculum has also allowed a strong case to be made for the importance of skill development to exam success in all subjects. Accordingly, cross-curricular literacy and numeracy initiatives have been introduced, and basic and key skills development has become the focus of skills days and pastoral lessons. Attention is also being paid to ensuring that the most able pupils are not allowed to 'drift', but are regularly challenged to achieve at ever higher levels.

Learning support for gifted and talented pupils

In addition to providing support for pupils with low literacy levels, the English department LSA at St Joseph's R.C. High School works with the most able and talented pupils at KS3. The intention is to provide these pupils with additional stimulus, so preventing them from simply cruising through their work. The school is committed to ensuring that these pupils reach their full potential.

The 30 most able Year 7 pupils are withdrawn from one English lesson per week following their examinations in the summer term. Texts covered by this group have included Ibsen's Doll's House and the poetry of Blake, and themes including the conflict between nature and technology and the portrayal of females in fiction have been addressed. A similar programme for Year 8 pupils runs from Easter until shortly before the summer examination period. Analysis of poetry, novels and plays is combined with discussion of works of art.

This supplements teachers' own classroom-based differentiation, which includes a specific focus on challenging able pupils. Departments from English and science to art have introduced more open-ended tasks, incorporating a greater range of key skills, and now supply the most talented pupils with additional tasks that stretch them beyond Key Stage 3 work ∎

A more comprehensive and consistent policy towards skill development has undoubtedly had a positive effect on pupil progress, but one innovation that stands out above all others is the introduction of mentoring for all pupils. Whilst two schools have introduced formally titled 'learning mentors' for every pupil, a third uses mentoring specifically for those pupils who are persistently underachieving. However, in all five schools there is at least one staff member who is overtly responsible for taking an overview of a pupil's progress.

Form tutors most often take on this role and can raise issues with pupils in daily registration periods or during dedicated tutorial times each half term. Reference to the comprehensive databases of pupil information or daily meetings between heads of year and form tutors provide the framework for these discussions. Mentors play an important consolidatory role, helping pupils to synthesise the information given to them by their subject teachers, reinforcing a message of success and ensuring that pupils are working consistently and effectively. This provides a constant drive for pupils to maintain an upward trajectory.

Early and widespread intervention

At Cwmtawe Community School, heads of year monitor pupil performance across all subjects on a termly basis. Spreadsheets are created on which are highlighted all subjects in which a pupil is above or below target. For pupils above target in four or more subjects, a letter of praise is sent home. Pupils below target in at least four subjects are the focus of a series of remedial actions.

Using the comprehensive array of data contained in the XL database, staff can ascertain possible causes for underachievement – including poor attendance, behavioural problems or lack of effort. Pupils with persistent problems, or who are underachieving in core subjects, are selected for mentoring. XL mentors are teachers who liaise with subject teachers and meet with the pupil once a week to address identified problems ∎

Key to the success of the case study schools in tackling underachievement is the adoption of an adaptable approach that can be tailored to the needs of a given intake or individual pupil. Strategies vary between schools, but also within schools over time, according to need. What unites these schools is not the particular responses that they make to underachievement or basic skills deficits. It is the existence of a consistently applied process for identifying those pupils in need, bringing together the relevant resources and putting into action the necessary strategies.

Balancing flexibility and accountability

As previously observed, each of the five features discussed above is characterised by its detailed and rigorous implementation, and by the time and energy that is applied to that implementation. Respondents were clear that the momentum generated by this approach is vital to sustaining progress. The demands placed on teachers are significant, but so is the satisfaction derived from improving outcomes for pupils. In each of the schools a shared ethos drives this commitment to achieving the best outcomes.

Critical to maintaining both teacher commitment and pupil progression are a creative approach to lessons and a flexible response to underachievement. Responsibility for identifying and implementing effective strategies is shared by all. The evidence presented here suggests that, for this to be successful, accountability structures must also be in place. It is interesting to note that strict application of accountability mechanisms does not preclude experimentation and creativity; rather, it serves to facilitate it. Similarly, relentless commitment to tackling underachievement goes hand in hand with flexibility of approach.

Whilst the schools share a focus on the five factors discussed above, the ways in which they put them into practice are highly varied. There is a need to safeguard the flexibility of approach which produces this variety. Every school is at a unique stage in its development, with different levels of success and facing specific local contexts and challenges. Each therefore requires an individualised strategy to improve further. To try to achieve this through a wholly centralised response would be ineffective. Just as schools exhibit trust in the ability of individual staff to identify appropriate strategies, so trust must be placed in professional capabilities at the whole-school level.

The case studies highlight a series of factors that are common to, at the very least, these successful schools. At the same time as having built an approach that encompasses these factors, they all acknowledge an ongoing need for innovation. The policy implications of the identified need to maintain this balance between structure and adaptability are discussed in the following chapter.

Chapter 5:
Policy implications

Judging by the Education Minister's recent pronouncement on the future of the Welsh education system[17], secondary education in Wales is on the cusp of rapid and substantial change. The response to Wales' poor performance in the 2009 PISA tests has been fierce and marked by reference to the 'simply shocking' basic skills of many young people, to 'system wide failures', and to the 'too cosy' relationship between government and educators. A powerful message is now being sent that the government will henceforth exert far greater control over the operation of our education system.

The government's response will drive towards: the application of minimum standards for schools; sharper accountability; the sharing of knowledge such that best practice becomes the standard; developing high quality teaching and leadership; and building system capacity, including through the institution of professional learning communities in all schools[18].

Each of these objectives is evident in the strategies of the successful schools profiled in this report. Policy changes that provoke more consistent adherence to them, and in so doing improve outcomes for all young people, are therefore to be welcomed. Nevertheless, the evidence suggests that caution will need to be exercised as regards the detail of their implementation.

The case studies presented here collectively provide insight into five issues addressed in the Minister's twenty proposed action points. These are: the decision to pursue a top twenty position in the 2015 PISA tests; the focus on monitoring and evaluation structures; the direction of continuing professional development; the planned implementation of annual pupil- and school-level targets; and increased attention to literacy and numeracy.

---

17   Leighton Andrews, 'Teaching makes a difference', 2 February 2011, Reardon Smith Lecture Theatre, National Museum of Wales, Cardiff.

18   Chris Tweedale, 14 February 2011, National Education Conference: Raising School Standards, Holland House Hotel, Cardiff.

Improving performance in PISA

Teachers have emphasised the beneficial impact of the skills-based curriculum on transition from Key Stage 2 to Key Stage 3. A shift in emphasis from the acquisition of knowledge to its application, which is much more in line with teaching at primary level, has occurred. The new curriculum was also praised for allowing far greater creativity in respect of teaching methods and lesson content; this contributes to teachers' ability to motivate pupils at a time when focus is particularly liable to wane. By contrast, the GCSE examination remains predominantly a test of pupils' ability to acquire knowledge. The resultant challenge of managing transition between learning styles from KS3 to KS4 was commonly acknowledged.

This finding has particular pertinence in light of the promised drive towards improved PISA performance. PISA measures ability to creatively apply prior knowledge to new situations. In the reading task pupils are expected to retrieve, interpret, reflect on and evaluate information found in a variety of texts. In mathematics, existing knowledge of mathematical concepts and methods is applied to real-world situations. The scientific survey assesses not only knowledge of scientific phenomena, but also awareness of context and ability to undertake the processes of scientific enquiry. Thus the purpose of PISA is to measure the extent to which pupils will be able to bring existing and new knowledge to bear in their adult lives[19].

Schools will now be expected to 'integrate PISA assessments into school assessment'[17]. This means that pupils who, in 2012, will be expected to meet the challenges of the PISA test will, less than a year later, be required to perform at GCSE. Given the highlighted tensions in the current KS3-KS4 transition, how much more challenging will it be to simultaneously prepare pupils for the GCSE test of the acquisition of knowledge and the PISA test of its application?

Should this dual focus be considered necessary then careful consideration will need to be given to how it will work in practice. Yet we must not seek to become accomplished in the PISA tests solely because we have previously failed to achieve highly in them. We must do so only if we believe PISA to be assessing something valuable. The 2008 introduction of the skills-based curriculum implied that we do hold ability to apply knowledge to

---

19   J. Bradshaw, R. Ager, B. Burge and R. Wheater, 2010, 'PISA 2009: Achievement of 15-year-olds in Wales', Slough: NFER.

be important. But ongoing testing at GCSE level of the acquisition of knowledge suggests that this, too, is seen to be valuable.

Pupils can excel in both the acquisition and application of knowledge, but unless this is an explicit goal it will be difficult to achieve consistency in the style and content of lessons throughout the course of a child's school career. It is insufficient simply to have targets that assess ability in a range of skill areas. In the case study schools, targets are underpinned by a shared ethos, a vision of what constitutes a well educated individual. It is this ethos that draws everything together and makes the difference between training pupils for a series of tests and educating them.

We have not yet seen significant public debate on the fundamental strategic direction of our education system. The question of what ends we desire from the education of our young people must be settled as a matter of urgency. This is not a question of having a mission statement or strategy document. It is a question of being absolutely clear about an end goal and consequent direction of travel. Only from such a strategic sense of purpose can a truly coherent and consistent system of education be formulated.

Monitoring and evaluation
The Education Minister has made it clear that he will 'have more direct input' to ensure that standards rise, and will 'be more prescriptive' when it comes to the content of continuing professional development[17]. In each of the case study schools rigorous and honest assessment of standards is already undertaken. Staff acknowledge that without it neither individual pupils nor the school as a whole would be able to progress.

Nevertheless, and despite past failures to rigorously monitor performance by some schools and at the system level, this does not justify the introduction of an overly prescriptive approach. To demand that all schools follow a process for monitoring and evaluating performance, and for implementing changes in light of that evaluation, is vital for improvement. To prescribe precisely what that process should look like and how it should operate would be as damaging as to continue with a laissez faire approach.

The case study schools' approaches to self-evaluation are highly differentiated. No two schools operate exactly the same system, and yet each school's monitoring and evaluation practices have been shown to be effective. These practices have been developed with reference to local context, such that each system operates in a way that makes use of the strengths of the staff whilst best ensuring ongoing development.

An overly prescriptive approach to monitoring performance and introducing positive change would risk undermining these existing, successful systems by imposing an additional and altogether separate burden of accountability. It would also be liable to generate unforeseen negative outcomes through the encouragement of gaming behaviour (as discussed below).

It is important that a framework is in place in every school to ensure that performance is regularly and rigorously monitored, progress assessed and appropriate measures to achieve progression implemented. As described in the previous chapter, the case study schools exhibited a number of common features in relation to their monitoring procedures. There can be, however, no one size fits all solution. Any national stipulations regarding schools' evaluation frameworks must be flexible enough to permit a diversity of approaches. If schools are to be required to share a rigid adherence to a set of monitoring protocols, the detail of how the protocols are implemented should be allowed to reflect local circumstances.

Placing trust in the professional judgement of the teachers and senior managers in our schools is not optional. Their detailed local knowledge makes them best placed to make decisions about their schools' development. Just as rigorous self-evaluation procedures within a school provide the evidence that allows senior management to trust in the decisions made by teachers, so external scrutiny processes will support the placing of trust in individual schools. Where schools are not yet performing sufficiently well to justify their having total control, a greater degree of external scrutiny and input can be introduced to the system.

Continuing professional development
As for evaluation procedures, so for continuing professional development. The Minister has stated that CPD 'will in future be focused on system-wide needs'[17]. Whilst there is a role for centrally-determined priorities, local context must be allowed to dictate at least part of the content of professional development. Teachers at different stages in their careers, with their own professional interests and working in environments with very particular challenges, will desire and need quite different forms of

professional development.

Excessive centralisation of the control of schools would hinder their improvement. The removal of decision-making powers from teachers and managers would deprofessionalise teaching, making it a far less attractive prospect to the most capable individuals. This is not to say that there is no role for central and local government. In respect of the workforce, the Welsh Government needs to make sure that there is a supply of high quality graduates for teaching and senior management posts. It also needs to guarantee funding to allow teachers to undertake continuing professional development and observe good practice elsewhere in the system. This will ensure that schools have the capacity to undertake rigorous evaluations and to plan and implement new strategies.

In addition, the government must find an appropriate balance between holding schools to account and giving them the freedom to innovate. Whilst greater accountability is vital if the Welsh school system is to move from 'fair to good'[17], implementation of overly rigid structures will prevent it from moving from 'good to great'. The example of Newtown High School, which has rapidly climbed from the 'serious weaknesses' category to a position of high value added, is perhaps the most striking in this regard. It provides evidence that, even in the early stages of improvement, a command and control approach is not the key to success. The government and local authorities should therefore work to facilitate capacity building within schools.

Judicious use of targets
The cases presented here are from some of Wales' best schools. To ensure that all schools are operating at this standard, proper scrutiny of their actions will be necessary. Local authorities should play an active role in the evaluation and development planning process. This should not entail a new set of reporting structures for schools, but rather should involve the extension of existing school-based monitoring beyond the school gate. In this context, local authorities would have a series of interconnected functions:

— To ensure that rigorously and regularly applied procedures for evaluating performance are in place within each school, and that these procedures are locally apposite. In some cases such procedures, or at least a less comprehensive version of them, will already be in place. In others, greater work will be required to bring a school to this point.

— To ensure that these procedures result in planned changes and outcomes over a set timescale, and to challenge schools when they do not.
— To be responsible for systematically sharing national priorities and good practice with all schools, and to ensure that schools maintain a balance between local and national priorities.

The overriding stance should be one of cooperation with schools. The case study examples demonstrate that it is possible to be both challenging and supportive, and that the environment thus created is conducive to generating and sustaining success. Within the case study schools, in the context of a rigorous monitoring framework that deals rapidly with underperformance, individuals can be given the freedom to exercise their professional judgement.

The indications are that the government plans to set targets centrally, against which all schools will be expected to perform. Targets have a part to play in any monitoring process, but they provide only a narrow indicator of success. If targets are the only means by which schools' trajectory and absolute standard are judged, the rational response will be to alter behaviour to meet them. There is, however, no guarantee that a response to these short term demands will be in the best interests of a school and its pupils in the longer term. Measurement against the newly proposed targets will be annual, whereas comprehensive Estyn inspections operate on a six year cycle. The potential for schools to modify behaviour to meet the targets, at the expense of longer term strategic development, is therefore high. To avoid short term gaming behaviour, targets should be used with extreme caution.

Furthermore, however carefully chosen the targets, a school's success cannot be reduced to performance against them. The case study schools' own monitoring procedures show just how complex and demanding a process it is to maintain an upward trajectory. The government must therefore consider how local authorities can be best equipped to develop detailed knowledge of the subtleties of their schools' performance and to engage in in-depth partnerships to support them.

Focusing on literacy and numeracy
The government's planned focus on literacy and numeracy mirrors efforts in the case study schools to ensure that all pupils have the skills necessary to access the curriculum. It must, however, be implemented with care, so as to avoid a return to an overly prescriptive curriculum.

The skills-based curriculum has been welcomed in the case study schools. Reduced prescription as regards lesson content has given teachers greater independence and allowed them to be more creative in their teaching. It has also encouraged greater cross-departmental working and improved pupil motivation. This latter benefit is of particular importance given the challenge of sustaining momentum during Key Stage 3.

As the case studies make clear, sustaining pupils' progression requires flexibility of approach in response to a nuanced understanding of individual needs. Needs vary not only between schools, but within schools over time. Excellent teachers are able to adapt their teaching methods at need, but must have a degree of autonomy to be able to do so.

Success in the case study schools has been built on the combination of a coordinated response to underachievement and a high level of creativity. Development of pupils' literacy and numeracy skills is critical, but must not be pursued at the expense of teachers' freedom to motivate and challenge their pupils. A balance must therefore be struck. A structured response to low literacy and numeracy levels must still allow schools the flexibility to simultaneously address other causes of underachievement.

Summation
Two forms of monitoring can be identified in relation to school performance. The first is the measurement of outcomes at the system level. This observation of what has been achieved makes reference to performance against predetermined targets. The second form of monitoring is of progression at the level of the individual pupil or school. This involves an ongoing assessment of how best to engender progress.

The first form of monitoring requires the definition of what outputs will be assessed and what targets must be met. For schools to be truly accountable, these must be defined and monitored centrally, by the government. By contrast, schools should ideally have the autonomy to determine how they will reach those targets, and what monitoring procedures are appropriate to that approach. It is through this autonomy that a balance between accountability and adaptability is achieved.

This research has identified two distinct policy responses that will be required in relation to these different kinds of monitoring. In terms of outcomes, the

Welsh Government must decide what it desires from our education system, and hence what outputs will be measured. At present we are, effectively by default, measuring performance using two quite different indicators, the GCSE and the PISA test. Going forward, there are three choices.

The government could decide to set the greatest store by the outcomes measured by GCSEs, and so ignore future PISA results. Alternatively, it could require all schools to perform in both GCSEs and PISA; given that the two tests have different focuses, this risks introducing confusion over what should be taught, and how, at Key Stages 3 and 4. Finally, the government could seek to embody the PISA philosophy within a compulsory baccalaureate-style qualification that would take the place of GCSEs. This is a difficult and grave decision. Whilst it absolutely must not be taken lightly, it will be necessary for the development of a consistent and effective education system.

Although the second form of monitoring, of progression, should ideally occur at the school level, the PISA results indicate that this level of autonomy is not yet justified for all schools. As our case studies show, some schools are already operating to a high standard. They undertake monitoring and evaluation that is suitable to their particular circumstances, and should be given the freedom to continue doing so. Others will need to earn that degree of autonomy. Schools which are not yet deploying and acting upon self-evaluation procedures with sufficient rigour will require external input. This does not mean that they should be required to renounce all control over the monitoring of school and pupil progression. The emphasis must be on building internal capacity, to enable ongoing development and allow the school to earn autonomy in the medium to long term.

Section 2:
Case studies

Chapter 6:
Cwmtawe Community School

School performance at KS3

Described in its 2006 inspection report as 'a good school with many outstanding features'[20], Cwmtawe Community School was found – using the KS2-KS3 contextual value added data for 2006-2008 – to be achieving results that, statistically speaking, are no different from those that would be expected of its pupils upon intake. This fact is duly acknowledged by the headteacher, who told us that at Cwmtawe 'the value added at Key Stage 3 is negligible':

> We look at the ability on intake and we look at the eventual outcomes. It's identical now to what it was eight years ago – no change. Eight years ago we were able to move them up to the level that we are still managing to maintain.

Thus, whilst expected progress is made between KS2 and KS3, there has been no increase in value added. Where the school does add value, however, is at KS4. Cwmtawe's results are significantly above the LEA and Welsh averages; the 2006-8 three year average of 76% of pupils achieving five or more GCSEs at A*-C is 14 points above the 2008/9 LEA level and 19 points above the 2008/9 all-Wales average[21]. Cwmtawe is therefore a school in which 'pupils of all abilities' make 'very good, and in some instances outstanding, progress'[20].

That pursuit of excellence principally at GCSE is a deliberate goal was made explicit by a number of our respondents. Members of the senior management team variously referred to KS3 as the 'grounding' or 'basis' for KS4, and

---

20   Estyn, 2006, Inspection under Section 28 of the Education Act 2005, Cwmtawe Comprehensive School.

21   Cwmtawe Community School, September 2009, Examination Performance and Annual Review 2009.

described how 'a large part of the work that's done at Key Stage 3 is preparation for GCSE'. This was a theme picked up in our discussions with members of the teaching staff, one of whom noted that 'we're measured on Key Stage 4 results, at the end of the day' and that this tended to relieve pressure at KS3 whilst focusing it on performance at KS4. This is not to say that concerted effort is not put into the teaching of KS3. Indeed, the need to maintain momentum between key stages, and to ensure that pupils meet their target grades throughout their time at Cwmtawe, means that there is 'an incredible amount of strategic focus' on Key Stage 3. The drive for continuous progression was also given as the reason why the headteacher had put in place two assistant headteachers, 'one in charge specifically of transition and Key Stage 3 [and] one specifically at Key Stage 4'.

The integration of all five years of KS3 and KS4 into a single progression at Cwmtawe is evidenced by the systems in place both for teaching pupils and for monitoring their progress. In respect of the former, Year 9 pupils effectively move into Year 10 – to begin their GCSE courses – at the start of the final half term of the summer, so giving them an extra six weeks of GCSE study. Whilst this might be expected to give pupils some advantage by allowing them to 'hit the ground running' at the beginning of the autumn term, it is the school's performance monitoring system, and the actions associated with it, that are regarded as contributing most effectively to the school's GCSE results. Indeed, this system is a most striking feature of the school's approach to raising performance.

Transition
Monitoring of pupils begins with their transition from the feeder primary schools. Both pastoral and pedagogic transition arrangements have developed over the past eight years, having been identified in the last three school development plans as a whole-school priority. Although work had been sent to the feeder schools from Cwmtawe for completion by Year 6 pupils for a number of years, this was originally used only as a way of 'ticking the right boxes'. Recognition of this has led to the development of a more interactive and innovative approach. Primary pupils are now invited to Cwmtawe to engage in activities throughout the year preceding their transition. A skills day is held in September, and transition projects focus on music or drama and sports. Each of these projects involves a visit to Cwmtawe – be it for a sports skills day or a musical performance for parents in the school hall – but also engages the feeder schools; following the sports

skills day, for example, primary teachers are given a scheme of work which they can use to promote ongoing skills development, whilst much of the preparation for the performance takes place within the primaries. Transition activities culminate with an induction day in July.

These activities play an important part in the pastoral transition of pupils into Year 7, since they give pupils 'a feel for the place', allowing them to familiarise themselves with staff and the school buildings. A key indicator of the success of these activities is that the pupils become 'fully engrossed' in them and 'forget where they are. When you walk around the school they're totally integrated [with pupils from other schools]'. However, as the shared schemes of work used for the transition projects suggest, the school also places a clear emphasis on pedagogic transition.

This area has received particular attention over the past eight years. Each of the school's feeder primaries now runs a series of themed sessions over the course of a week during the summer term, in order to facilitate a more 'seamless' pedagogic transition into Year 7. These sessions – which in recent years have included *CSI Cwmtawe* science activities and a *Spirit of Cwmtawe* treasure hunt, described by one respondent as 'innovative, interactive 'skills' adventure activities' – require the application of a range of skills and methods to the solution of a series of problems. By solving all the clues presented to them, pupils work to solve a mystery. Staff at Cwmtawe have put considerable effort into creating video, audio and textual resources specifically for the projects; these are made available to the primary schools in a resource pack and through access to a dedicated website or use of a DVD.

The transition projects represent a shift away from 'traditional' transition projects: they are cross-curricular rather than subject-based; and their structure, comprising a series of tasks which contribute to the solution of a mystery, encourages pupils to reflect on their progress at each stage and to make connections between tasks. Pupils benefit from these projects through their exposure to a range of key skills and through the early introduction of concepts that they will encounter during Year 7, such as chromatography or six-figure grid referencing. The projects also introduce Key Stage 2 teachers to concepts and methods employed at Key Stage 3, and hence aid continuity of teaching between the key stages.

Sharing of data, schemes of work and teaching strategies is considered central to the effective pedagogic transition of Cwmtawe's pupils, and accordingly a meeting is held every half term with the primary school headteachers. In addition, meetings are held three times per year with Year 6 teachers for the purpose of standardisation and moderation of pupils' work. In the past year the cluster has been focusing on moderation of individual pupils' portfolios, and Cwmtawe has also organised whole-cluster Inset days on the implementation of literacy, numeracy, ICT and skills strategies across the curriculum. The local authority was identified as having been an important partner, having served to link local and national agendas and delivered training sessions which have aided development of a transition programme that takes good account of the skills framework.

Additional subject-specific transition activities are necessarily undertaken on a school-by-school basis because, in addition to Cwmtawe's thirteen feeder primaries, of which seven are Welsh primaries which send pupils to a mix of English and Welsh medium schools, the school attracts pupils from twenty schools through preferred placement. Since each of these schools is likely to send the majority of its pupils to schools other than Cwmtawe, it is often impractical to engage with them on specific transition projects.

Cwmtawe makes use of a wide range of data. The school has an assistant headteacher with responsibility for KS3 who, together with other key colleagues, works closely with the thirteen feeder primaries. Data requested on each pupil include records of attendance, homework completion and behaviour, information on what, if any, additional support the pupil is receiving, and notes on sporting and musical abilities. This allows the school to build a picture of the pupil as a whole prior to his or her arrival at Cwmtawe, and assists with the banding of pupils on entry and with the assignment of support for those in need.

Teacher assessments are also received, and staff at Cwmtawe note that the pupils whose Key Stage 2 teacher assessment fails to match the cognitive abilities test (CAT) score achieved at the start of Year 7 are 'few and far between'. The headteacher's judgement is that:

> there has been a reluctance on behalf of our thirteen feeder
> schools to jump through hoops to gain accreditation at the higher
> level. So we have thirteen schools that have stuck to the norm.

Thus, in spite of 'external pressure put on them to increase their results', the primaries are not distorting the teacher assessments upwards, allowing

Cwmtawe to trust in the information that is being sent to them for Year 6 pupils.

XL @ Cwmtawe

One highly developed aspect of the school is its monitoring system, known as XL@Cwmtawe. This encompasses pupil effort, achievement and behaviour, and allows for the ready sharing of information on these between subject teachers, form tutors and senior management.

The data requested from the feeder primaries – in paper format on a standard form, thus minimising the administrative burden on teachers – include information on achievement, attendance, homework completion, support received and behaviour. Teacher assessments are given by level, with the addition of 'high', 'mid' or 'low' to distinguish between pupils within levels. These data form the basis of a database of pupil data that is used throughout Years 7-11. Two elements of this system are considered critical to its success.

Firstly, each pupil is given a single target grade for all subjects in Year 7. This is based on pupils' KS2 teacher assessment levels and CAT test results, and is assigned towards the end of the first term. The targets were described as 'far higher' than one would normally expect:

> A child coming in here might get a C grade target in most schools. We give them a B grade target, and they have to hit the B grades. If they don't get it, at Key Stage 3 or Key Stage 4, they have a mentor put in.

Senior staff believe that by setting the target this high – at least one grade ahead of that suggested by a pupil's CAT score – pupils are challenged more than might be the case in many other schools. The 'simplicity' of using a single grade is regarded as crucial to the system's effectiveness:

> Pupils have got a standard target grade. ... It's kind of saying "there's the bar – now you've got to keep trying to jump over that".

This appealed to the pupils to whom we spoke. One Year 9 pupil described the system as 'quite easy to follow', and there was agreement among the pupils that they prefer to be pushed to try harder. When asked to consider the difference between a 'good' and a 'bad' lesson, one pupil explained that she preferred to be able to see rapid progression through a course, so as to avoid lessons that feel 'just so long'.

An additional benefit of the single grade target is that, as a constant reminder of the highest standard that a pupil is expected to be capable of, it guards against the underestimation of pupil ability, by pupils or teachers, in individual subject areas. Performance in *any* subject that fails to meet this high standard will be flagged as *under*performance.

Part of the refinement of the monitoring system that has occurred during the twelve years of its operation has involved the sharing of target grades with pupils. Pupils were previously told only whether they were above, on or below target, but this complicated conversations with them about how to improve. Feedback has also been improved. Following one pupil noting that she did not understand how she had moved from below to on target in a particular subject, stickers were introduced for teachers to place in pupils' school diaries. These have printed on them the XL@Cwmtawe classroom rules:

— Come equipped
— Complete classwork to the best of your ability
— Complete all homework and hand it in on time
— Concentrate on your work and don't disturb others
— Respect your teacher, classmates and school property

Teachers can place a tick alongside any rule that a pupil needs to focus on, and can add subject-specific advice and targets. This example suggests that, although our discussions with pupils indicated that the School Council does not provide a formal mechanism for sharing *academic* concerns (as opposed to issues of a more pastoral nature), informal mechanisms for pupil input do exist. Plans are in place to further develop opportunities for pupils to become involved in curricular issues.

The second key element of the system is the banding of pupils, based on KS2 teacher assessments, into broad ability groups. Banding is employed in preference to mixed ability groups. According to the school's assistant headteacher for KS3:

> if we took the banding system away, none of the other things we do would work.

Indeed, Cwmtawe staff have, in the past, visited a school – one of a number to have shown interest in implementing a similar target and monitoring system – where it was felt that that school's mixed ability classes would make it 'virtually impossible' to make the system work. By teaching in broad ability bands, teachers are better able to ensure that *all* pupils are challenged academically, without going so far as to pigeonhole pupils at the beginning of their secondary school career.

Cwmtawe has a nine form entry, comprising:

— five top bands;
— one 'bridging' group, which undertakes top band work but at a slower pace and in which pupils have a C/D borderline target grade (equating to a low level 4);
— two smaller second band classes of approximately 22 pupils, each working at about level 3; and
— one special educational needs (SEN) class.

Performance in each of these classes is monitored on a termly basis. The use of computer-based records was not without resistance in the early days of its implementation, from teachers used to a previous paper-based system. However, a firm commitment from senior staff to ensuring that all teachers use the system, combined with a clear focus on the application of the data – rather than collection of data for data's sake – appears to have paid dividends.

The importance of collecting these data was highlighted by all of the teachers interviewed. The school was described as being 'very data rich', which was variously considered as aiding 'teacher focus' and helping to ensure that 'we don't miss anyone out. A lot of pupils in the top band get reading support'. (This link between data collection and action to address underachievement is discussed in the following section.) In the history department a single spreadsheet is used to allow ongoing checking of grades, allowing teachers to focus lessons on specific areas in which pupils require extra help. Meanwhile a technology teacher noted that the system is particularly useful in her subject: pupils move on to a different topic, with a different teacher, each six weeks, but the availability of data from previous teachers' lessons gives each new teacher a good indication of a pupil's current standard from the outset.

One other reason for the success of the computer-based system appears to be that it is highly efficient. It has not required teachers to spend valuable time on data entry and the learning of complicated new technologies associated with it. Although the data are presented on screen, subject teachers continue to complete paper forms detailing pupil effort and achievement. These data are then read onto computer and presented back to staff in a user-friendly format, minimising the administrative demands made of them.

Close attention is also paid to pupil behaviour. This has improved substantially since the school's move to its current site. According to one teacher who has been at Cwmtawe for fifteen years:

> the results were poor when I joined. As soon as we moved to this building ... you could see the significant improvement straight away. I'd only been up in the other school for one year ... but it was just the atmosphere – kids moving from lesson to lesson, they could hide away and not get to lessons, and it was difficult for the teachers and for the senior management just to control the flow of children. ... And if anything happened in lessons, I was teaching in one building [and] my head of department was ... nearly half a mile away.

The school has been on its present site since 1996, during which time the XL@Cwmtawe system has been developed. Infringements of the classroom or general school rules – from failure to arrive on time or bring the appropriate equipment to lack of respect for others – can be noted immediately by subject teachers using the system. This information is available to form tutors, who raise the issue with pupils during registration, and can be monitored on a daily and weekly basis by heads of year. Teachers described a system of escalation from the classroom, through department heads and heads of year to senior management, depending upon the seriousness of the infringement. The intention is that low-level disruption is dealt with by each department, with repeated infringements passed to the head of department, who will liaise with the head of year. Serious issues can be referred directly to the senior management team.

Those pupils interviewed seemed well aware not only of the existence of the school rules but also of the need to follow them. One Year 7 pupil commented that:

teachers have to be a little bit strict because they need discipline to teach well. If there's no discipline, there's no point teaching.

This was a view supported by pupils in Year 9, with pupils from all three year groups agreeing that XL@Cwmtawe is a policy that they see being put into practice. Bullying, for example, is 'taken really seriously': a pupil found to have bullied others is expected to sign a form explaining the nature of his or her actions, which is kept on the pupil's file for a set period of time.

Addressing underachievement

Whilst the management at Cwmtawe have created a comprehensive monitoring system, they are at pains to emphasise that the purpose is not 'just to run numbers' but to produce useful data, in a usable format, that can aid in improving pupil performance. One head of year, who 'absolutely loves' the system and described it as 'fantastic', explained how he uses the data each term.

A spreadsheet showing each pupil's performance in every subject allows for a swift overview of achievement, with subjects in which the pupil is above target highlighted in green and those in which he or she is below target in orange. The parents of pupils with four or more subjects above target are sent a letter of praise. For the term prior to our visit, letters were sent for 122 out of 240 pupils. Those pupils with four or more subjects below target are subject to further scrutiny. Attendance data are checked, subject teachers are consulted for information on behaviour, and effort levels are examined. This gives the head of year a good indication of the nature of the problem, prompting a series of follow-up actions. Firstly, a letter is sent to the pupil's parents, detailing the concern and asking them to come in to the school. If the parents fail to respond, the head of year will telephone, again asking the parents for a meeting. Should they decline this, the head of year will discuss the issues over the telephone. Parents do engage with the school but, following attendance of around 75% at the first parents' evening of Year 7, there is some dip in engagement. In cases where parents do not attend, subject teachers or heads of year will again make further efforts to make contact.

Whilst every effort is made to engage parents, the system is designed to aid pupils even in the absence of parental support. Thus the second response to underachievement is for the head of year, in consultation with the assistant headteacher for KS3, to draw up a list of pupils requiring mentoring. Not all pupils can be mentored, so priority is given to pupils underachieving in core subjects or where longer term problems – rather than, for example, underachievement due to recent bereavement – are evident. XL mentors are teachers who receive regular updates from subject teachers, and meet weekly with mentored pupils to address the problems identified. Pupils carry a record book in which concerns, progress and actions are recorded. Mentors also liaise with parents on a weekly basis where possible.

Described as a 'catch-all system', in which even pupils with an A grade target who are getting Bs will be considered for mentoring, the system is designed to ensure that even the most able pupils are not allowed to 'drift'. This was described by one respondent as a key difference from mentoring schemes in other schools. The integration of achievement, effort and behaviour records was considered to result in a more nuanced understanding of the reasons for underachievement, allowing for a comprehensive approach to tackling it.

Literacy and numeracy support
Clearly, in addition to poor behaviour, effort or attendance, low literacy and numeracy can play a significant part in limiting achievement. The school's numeracy and literacy coordinators both sit on a working group that is seeking 'to move the school forward' on skills development, and the coordinators disseminate any information that they think is necessary to subject teachers. The numeracy and literacy coordinators also make themselves available to any teacher requiring advice or support for their lessons, although they are rarely asked to assist other teachers. Once a week in registration pupils work on numeracy booklets, and the mathematics schemes of work have also been altered to increase emphasis on numeracy tasks, including number bonds, times tables and adding numbers between one and twenty.

By comparison, literacy support is far more developed. Described by an assistant headteacher as 'intense', the literacy support in place from the outset of Year 7 was identified by the literacy coordinator as being 'one of the major reasons that people progress'. The school's focus on literacy from day one of Year 7 was attributed to the intervention of the headteacher. One respondent described how, when the headteacher first arrived, he had identified pupils at Key Stage 4 who had reading difficulties. To address this, he assigned learning support assistants (LSAs) specifically to those pupils. This prompted a subsequent shift to the targeted use of LSAs at a far earlier stage, to prevent pupils from reaching Key Stage 4 without sufficient literacy skills.

The importance of early identification and targeting of low literacy was raised by both teachers and senior management, with the philosophy that 'if you're literate you can access the curriculum' being mentioned on more than one occasion. As one respondent explained it, 'when you talk about pupils dipping off, what's happening to them is they come into secondary school without the skills of reading to access the curriculum'. That this is true across the curriculum has apparently been widely taken on board. According to the school's literacy coordinator:

> as a staff, people are very, very clued in to the fact that, if they improve pupils' literacy in their subject, ultimately they will get better outcomes at Key Stage 4.

Support is provided for all pupils with a reading age of less than ten years by the special educational needs department, which comprises 16 learning support assistants and two special educational needs (SEN) teachers. A past increase in resources, bringing with it a growth in the number of LSAs, has allowed a greater number of pupils to be targeted: previously only pupils with a reading or spelling age below nine received support. Pupils receive support in registration time or pastoral lessons, with withdrawal from other lessons being avoided if at all possible. Groups of approximately fifteen children go to the SEN department during registration and are taught through a programme of buddy reading between Year 7s and the brightest Year 9s, reading groups and use of the SuccessMaker software and SRA reading cards.

The special educational needs coordinator (SENCO) and literacy coordinator are both focused on providing support 'for as many pupils as we can', regardless of the class in which they have been placed; between one third and one half of all pupils receive support at some stage during KS3, and approximately 40-50% of pupils receiving literacy support are in the top band. Because almost half of each year group, including a large number of top band pupils, visit the SEN department, there is 'not a stigma' attached to getting help. Key Stage 3 pupils to whom we spoke, although not necessarily overly enamoured of receiving support – because it 'can be boring sometimes' – thought that it had been beneficial, and all were happy to discuss having received help. Virtually 100% of pupils who are assisted with their literacy can be expected to reach a reading age of ten or above by the end of Year 9, at the age of 14, with the majority reaching this point by Year 8.

Funding of the learning support assistants comes from 'whatever the head can get his hands on', and the greatest threat to the ongoing success of the literacy support system therefore appears to be from uncertainty over funding going forward. The system is highly dependent on the number of staff available:

> Lots of other people would want to do the same ... as we're doing, but if you haven't got the staff to do it, if you haven't got the support assistants to do it, you can't.

This uncertainty led to a 'worry that you're not going to be able to do so much in the future' being expressed. Already the number of withdrawals from lessons has been reduced, with a greater focus on in-class support from LSAs and more use made of registration and break times. Given that the norm is to provide literacy support only for pupils with a reading age below nine, it remains possible that Cwmtawe will have to revert to this level of support. The situation at Cwmtawe has been made possible only because resource levels are currently sufficient to allow it but, with the financial 'juggling act' seeming likely to continue, one respondent noted that 'we've just got to work harder then at what we're doing to try and make sure that those results come'.

Basic skills
During lesson time, the school's SEN team focuses on providing support to pupils with additional educational needs. The number of pupils receiving School Action or School Action Plus or with statements has risen in recent years, to 28% of the student body. This was attributed to an increase in the number of pupils from outside the catchment whose parents send them to Cwmtawe 'because they've heard that [the SEN department] can work wonders with their children'.

Whilst the funding coming to the department is largely based on the number of statemented pupils at the school, the SENCO works 'on the assumption [that] if that kid needs it we've got to do it', regardless of whether or not he or she has a statement. Thus although LSAs are often assigned to a specific statemented pupil within a class, it is anticipated that 'other children will benefit' from their presence in the classroom. At present, each of the bottom three classes in Year 9 has an assistant in the class for virtually every lesson. In Years 7 and 8 the same is true for the bottom class.

Basic skills lessons have also taken on an increasingly important role in raising the standards of the lower groups. All Key Stage 3 pupils in the two second band classes and in the SEN class – effectively every pupil with a level 3 on entry in Year 7 – are disapplied from either French or German and take two basic skills lessons per week in its place. A combination of group work and individual programmes is followed in these lessons, and frequent retesting is used to monitor progress. The smaller size of these classes, each of which numbers approximately 22 pupils, makes it 'much easier' to focus on improving the basic skills. Some of these lessons are taken by the headteacher, suggesting high-level recognition of the importance of basic skills to future achievement.

Pupil wellbeing

Staff at Cwmtawe believe that the XL@Cwmtawe system ensures that underachievement is addressed among all pupils, regardless of its root cause. Consequently, the school does not have specific policies in place to support looked after children or those from deprived backgrounds: each case is assessed independently and support provided accordingly. Central to this support are the assistant heads of year, who are the designated looked after children (LAC) coordinators. As well as acting as the XL mentor for any looked after children in their year, they attend all of the multi-agency meetings that relate to those pupils.

The commitment of staff towards pupils was specifically mentioned by the headteacher, who argued that teachers' work with pupils outside lesson time makes a significant difference. Pupils also picked up on this. When asked what the best things about Cwmtawe are, they said:

> Teachers offer you help if you don't understand what they mean.

and:

> At lunchtime and outside of school they agree to give up their time.

One assistant headteacher described pupils as being 'totally surrounded' by support 'from below' – by the special needs department and the literacy and numeracy coordinators – and 'from above' – by the senior management team and heads of year. This is particularly beneficial for those pupils who lack support at home, many of whom it is possible for the SENCO to identify:

> Now I'm in the situation with a lot of the children where I taught their parents. So you know them, they know you. ... You know ... what they're going home to ... and you think "well, if we don't do it and put it in there, it won't get done". So we do it.

As a result, 'when the children come here they do feel cared for ... They find their home down with us. And that really, then, is just what makes them come on as much as the time you spend reading with them'.

Heads and assistant heads of year have both pastoral and curricular responsibilities, but the latter have increasingly taken priority. A recent development that has helped to redress this balance is the use of peer mentors. These are pupils, many of whom have encountered their own problems early in their time at Cwmtawe, who have received training in listening and questioning techniques. The mentors have contact with heads of year and the assistant headteacher for pupil welfare, and will share concerns of a serious nature with them, but provide a potential first port of call for other pupils who are experiencing difficulties.

Leadership and future strategy
A number of statements made by senior management in relation to teaching staff at Cwmtawe suggested that a significant degree of trust is present. The headteacher, for example, whilst aware that KS3 English results had dropped into the bottom quartile for the LEA in the current year, explained that the department attributed this to the ability level of that year group. He then went on to state that it would be easy for him to push the department on their results, the unstated implication being that he did not consider this necessary given the department's explanation. It is possible that this level of trust is underpinned by the existence of XL@Cwmtawe: the richness of the data allows for a nuanced understanding of cause and effect, and so potentially reduces the temptation to micromanage.

Similarly, as already noted, members of the senior management team discussed the Key Stage 2 teacher assessment results from the feeder primaries in positive terms, reporting that the assessed levels closely correlate with results from the cognitive abilities tests (CATs) undertaken by pupils at the beginning of Year 7. This ongoing consistency is clearly valued at Cwmtawe and, where greater standardisation of levels is deemed necessary, staff feel able to address this in unison with the primaries.

The delegation of responsibilities to members of the senior management team was also described as an important factor in the school's ongoing success and future development. The headteacher has given each member of the SMT a specific area of responsibility, because he believes that the strengths of all team members can be brought to bear in a way that would not be possible if he required the final say on every decision. Furthermore, an emphasis has been placed on succession management within the school. With the exception of the headteacher, all members of the SMT were appointed from within Cwmtawe and, having experienced the system as teachers, are well placed to suggest how best it might be developed in future.

One question that remains at Cwmtawe concerns what changes will be necessary to move KS3 performance on from its current static position. The senior management team relayed discussions that they have been having regarding the introduction of different subjects to the Key Stage 4 curriculum and the possibility of limiting the number of GCSE options for less able pupils, so that they are not required to study a 'full', and overly challenging, quota of ten subjects. These are contested issues which have not yet been resolved. Concerns include whether alternative subjects could fail to meet the 'gold standard' of existing subjects, and how it can be ensured that pupils are not prevented from following subjects that they enjoy. Schools in this study with significant value added at Key Stage 3 highlighted the importance of creating a consensus to take the school forward and so, provided that they are resolved into a shared vision for its next steps, these debates at Cwmtawe would seem to have a valuable function.

It was clear that the teachers to whom we spoke had been redesigning schemes of work in light of the skills-based curriculum and to better prepare pupils for Key Stage 4. The discussions we had suggested that the new curriculum and the removal of formal assessment at Key Stage 3 were valued for allowing teachers greater control over the curriculum and 'that little bit more freedom' to choose how the course is taught. Emphasis is placed on preparing children for Key Stage 4 courses – in line with the clear school-wide view of KS3 as a building block for KS4. A similar need to address continuity between KS2 and KS3 was also acknowledged by teachers to whom we spoke. One described the changing nature of lesson structures in primary schools:

> There's a lot more little group work and pair work and three work in primary school. Certainly they don't get taught [this subject] in a traditional way as a whole class, all doing the same together. They work in little groups at different times. And that seems to be quite a common approach for them, where they're all working almost individually.

Meanwhile her colleague highlighted the importance of maintaining consistency of learning styles between the primary schools and Cwmtawe:

> I think that in Key Stage 2 now there's such a different learning style, and I think we've got to really take that on board. Because I think that the children coming in are used to doing things in a different way, and I don't know if they therefore respond so much to the traditional approach.

Whilst there was some indication that certain teachers felt that they had not yet moved sufficiently beyond this 'traditional' approach, members of the senior management team drew attention to the school's 'sector leading' transition arrangements and to the priority placed on the creation of new schemes of work in response to the skills-based curriculum.

The trust that Cwmtawe has developed in its feeder schools provides a strong platform for the development of curricular links. In addition, Cwmtawe's 14-19 curriculum has undergone recent changes, which include the introduction of a BTEC in construction in partnership with Neath College and the establishment in 2010 of courses in hairdressing, sport, hospitality and catering, and leisure and tourism, as well as BTEC business. As they become embedded at KS4, there is the potential for teaching methods associated with these more practical courses to influence practice at KS3. From the innovative KS2-KS3 transition projects already in place it is evident that staff at Cwmtawe are open to the possibilities presented by curricular developments in other key stages, and will be willing to put into practice such strategies as are necessary to further enhance performance.

Chapter 7:
Newtown High School

School performance at KS3

Described in its most recent Estyn inspection report as 'a good school with several outstanding features', Newtown High School has seen significant and rapid improvement. The school was placed in the 'serious weaknesses' category following an earlier inspection in 2003 but, following the appointment of a new headteacher and an influx of new staff, it is regarded as having made 'outstanding' improvements[22].

Contextual value added from Key Stage 2 to Key Stage 3 was, for the three years 2006-2008, positive at a significant level. In 2008, the proportion of pupils achieving Level 5 or above in English at Newtown was nine points higher than the national average. In mathematics this gap was 10.7 points, and in science 4.9 points. Overall, 66.9% of pupils achieved the core subject indicator, 7.3% more than did so nationally[22].

Newtown has also made rapid progress at Key Stage 4. Staff reported that approximately one third of pupils reached the Level 2 threshold at the time of the 2003 inspection, compared with nearly three quarters of pupils today. The school is 'ambitiously' aiming for 100% of pupils to reach this standard in the coming year, and has begun to introduce a range of qualifications in addition to GCSEs to assist them. Many of these are being introduced at Key Stage 3, and are discussed below.

School leadership

The headteacher was consistently cited by staff as being the principal catalyst for these developments. Upon appointment, she introduced the concept of 'CYFLE' as the underpinning ethos for the school. As well as

---

22   Esytn, 2009, Inspection under Section 28 of the Education Act 2005,
        A Report on the Quality of Education in Newtown High School.

being Welsh for 'opportunity', CYFLE stands for 'Caring Yields a Flourishing Learning Environment'. According to one member of the senior management team, 'if you care enough things *will* come good'. This belief, coupled with an absolute 'determination' not to let students down, drives everything that the school does for its students. It has also brought about a change in focus: 'the school isn't run for the teachers... [It's] now run very much for the success of the students.'

Staff who had been present throughout this period of improvement noted that it had not come about 'overnight', but had taken many years and a lot of 'very, very hard work by everybody'. Three factors were highlighted by staff as being central to the successful turnaround of the school, namely the foregrounding of challenge as a key concept for staff and pupils, the development of middle management and the implementation of a rigorous self-evaluation process.

The importance to staff of challenging themselves, their students and each other was described as having been 'ingrained in all of us' by the headteacher. This culture of constant challenge feeds a 'can-do attitude' and ensures that staff are 'always moving forward' and seeking ways to improve. At root, its aim is to ensure that:

> we do not let [pupils] down. If they are capable of this then that is what they will get. We make sure that they get that.

This ethos is apparent in the use of individualised targets for all pupils and the introduction of Level 2 qualifications at Key Stage 3, both of which are described in detail below. It is also evident in teachers' approach to their own continuing professional development.

Staff are encouraged by the headteacher to seek out and visit schools showing evidence of good practice in their field. In addition, the headteacher, who was described as being 'very well informed', will point specific teachers in the direction of good practice that she has encountered during her own visits to other schools. Inset days and twilight sessions are used to share and debate new ideas. Staff are encouraged to trial new approaches. In one example given by a teacher, following an external course on the use of success criteria and peer assessment, staff were consulted and an appropriate approach was developed for use at Newtown. This determination to seek out and implement the best available practice has been instrumental in Newtown's success. Respondents described a number of initiatives which originated in other schools but have now become central to the Newtown approach. These include the system for monitoring whether pupils are on, above or below target.

The second key strand in the development of leadership at the school has been an increased focus on the role of middle managers. Firstly, an extended senior leadership team (ESLT) has been created. Young members of staff who are new to the profession, and who are working on the iNet Developing Leaders for Tomorrow programme, have been brought into the ESLT to contribute 'new, sparky ideas' to the school. Secondly, whilst senior management retain responsibility for monitoring overall pupil and departmental progress, heads of department have control over the day-to-day running of their departments. One respondent noted that, with the introduction of the self-evaluation process, heads of department have recently 'had to take more responsibility'.

Clear lines of communication exist – and are used – between teachers, the heads of department and each head of department's link manager in the senior management team. As one head of department commented:

> ... everybody knows what's going on. Nothing is kept from us and we don't keep anything from our staff. There's communication all the way. So the senior leadership are very good at sharing with us at middle leadership level what their vision is, what they want us to do, what their expectations are.

Expanding on this, a second departmental head explained that these lines of communication are not simply top-down, but work both ways:

> [Senior management] also listen to us. If I go to my link manager or the Head and ... [say] I think we should be doing this, I'm listened to. And quite often I get what I've requested. So I feel valued, and that helps.

Equally, heads of department trust in the abilities of their departments' teachers. An important advantage of this is that heads can delegate responsibility for trialling new initiatives to others. This allows far more innovations to be assessed, and potentially implemented, than would be the case if middle managers felt unable to devolve responsibility. The self-evaluation process, with its clear lines of accountability, acts as a rigorous monitoring system that makes the initial development of such trust far easier.

Self-evaluation framework

Progress in each department is measured against a 'common yardstick' in the form of an ongoing cycle of self-evaluation. The system, introduced by the current headteacher, was variously represented by staff as being 'very thorough', 'incredibly useful' and 'rigorous'. Although having considered her previous school to be 'quite innovative' in its self-evaluation procedures, one teacher reported how much more in-depth the Newtown system is. It is based on Estyn's inspection criteria, which have been filtered by the headteacher and turned into a forty-page grid. Not all parts are universally relevant, and departments address only those issues that relate to their work. Although it was described as 'quite daunting when you first look at it', the grid is designed in a 'user-friendly' way and guides staff through the evaluation.

Each department receives a copy of the grid in September. With reference to the previous year's evaluation and examination results, a new evaluation takes place. The grid is then used as a working document throughout the year and tends to be on the agenda at most faculty meetings. Emphasis is placed on undertaking an honest assessment of where each department currently stands, and departments are expected to demonstrate where and how they are progressing. To this end, findings from the self-evaluation feed into faculty and departmental improvement plans.

Meetings are held between heads of department and their link managers in the senior management team, at which self-evaluation reports, improvement plans and examination results are discussed. Where targets have been missed this must be justified, and low pupil attainment must be explained 'almost down to the [level of the] individual child'. The thoroughness of the data interrogation means that teachers 'make sure that [they] have the answers'.

However, although staff are 'not let off' if targets are not met, 'there's no big stick'. In one head of department's words:

> I know there's lots of [targets] that I haven't hit but there's lots
> of things that I have hit. ... I'm a manager and I manage my time
> and prioritise. So if I haven't managed to do those I'll just change

the timescale. Because we're valued as professionals, for our professional judgement ... I'll say I haven't been able to do this because of this, and I need this to do it. And I've always been supported.

The importance of this positive and supportive approach to self-evaluation was emphasised by respondents. Given that, as one acknowledged, 'without being open and honest about where you actually are you're never ... going to improve', the need to be able to discuss progress without fear of being reprimanded is vital.

Although the very first self-evaluation in particular was relatively time consuming, now that staff can modify a working document the time commitment has been reduced. Ultimately, however, the time involved need not be an issue if the returns are sufficiently high. Most, if not all, staff were believed to have welcomed rigorous self-evaluation 'because they can see it as a way forward'. It also appears that self-evaluation has aided cross-departmental engagement. According to one respondent it is notable that, unlike seven years ago, 'everybody is singing from the same hymn sheet now'. All departments use the same self-evaluation grid and 'do talk to each other' about it.

Target setting and challenge
According to one respondent:

>...children's attitude to learning has changed completely. So they are motivated now to want to succeed. Before it wasn't cool to succeed. Now it is cool to succeed.

This change in attitude has been brought about through use of 'aspirational' targets. All targets are set by the headteacher and her deputy. Pupils have separate targets for each subject, which are based on past performance and cognitive abilities test (CAT) scores. Each target has 'a bit of bite ... a bit of ambition in there' and, whilst heads of department can raise a target, 'they have to argue very, very hard to bring them down'.

Because targets are underpinned by data showing what a pupil is capable of, expectations – of students and staff – are raised:

It's getting rid of those ... attitude barriers, in terms of "oh well, it's Newtown, what do you expect?". ... No, this is what they're capable of and that's what we're going to get. And I think that's what you'll hear from the other staff. The bar's up there now.

Further challenge is provided by the 'NTU' system. Each half term, pupils are recorded as being 'U': under target, 'T': on target, or 'N': achieving at 'Newtown standard', or above target. That the targets are school-wide was welcomed by one respondent, who reported that:

> we've set targets in [this subject] going back fifteen years. We were always [looking at] the CAT scores, the levels they come in at, [and then saying] this is what they need to have by the end of Key Stage 3. But I don't think it was until it became whole-school that it really had an impact.

This whole-school approach extends to addressing issues with performance as they arise. One respondent, a parent and administrative staff member, had found that 'there seems to be so much communication. ... You can see where something's going wrong and somebody, somewhere will pick up on it.' Action is then taken to rectify the problem. An example was cited of an otherwise high-performing pupil whose performance slipped to a 'U' in one subject. This was picked up on 'straightaway' by the school and the family. An appointment was made for the family to meet with the head of year, all staff were emailed requesting information on the pupil, and suitable catch-up work was set. This whole process took less than a week.

Teachers agreed that pupils value the NTU system and are now genuinely concerned when they are underachieving. Whereas 'U's were a 'badge of honour' when first introduced, now 'even the kids who pretend they don't care do care'. That high expectations are placed on pupils was confirmed by those to whom we spoke, one of whom said:

> We're told that ['Newtown standard'] is the standard we should be hitting, more than 'on target'. If we go for that standard it's going to be better all round. ['On target'] is seen as [only] a satisfactory standard.

Assessment and progression

These pupils were well aware of what to do to improve their performance. They described how their tutors direct them to speak to teachers in subjects where they are underperforming, and showed an example of a student planner, in which they record targets, actual performance and teachers' advice.

The role of the form tutor has become increasingly important in recent years. Tutors now also act as learning mentors. Mentors receive a full set of NTU grades each term and will sit down with each pupil to discuss them. If the pupil is below target, he or she will be directed to the relevant subject teachers to find out why. Pupils who are on target will discuss with the mentor how they might improve further, whilst those with subjects above target will consider what they have done differently to achieve these higher grades. The benefits of mentoring were described by one head of department as being that:

— it keeps pupils focused;
— it motivates pupils who receive little or no support at home; and
— it ensures that all pupils are progressing in the right direction.

As mentors are also form tutors, they have time in both registration periods and personal and social education (PSE) lessons to work with the pupils.

Formal assessments play a key role in determining pupils' progress and are carried out on a termly basis. These are placed on the school calendar to highlight their importance. Information from the assessments is fed back to senior management, who maintain an overview and ensure that all assessments are being carried out. Marks are awarded separately in each area of assessment – for example in knowledge, understanding and ability to evaluate in R.E., or speaking, reading, writing and listening in Welsh. This allows teachers to regularly assess an individual pupil's weaknesses and address them in future lessons. Assessments are also used as an opportunity to engage pupils in their progression towards the end of the key stage. If a pupil is aiming for Level 7 in Year 9, he or she can work out what percentage is needed in tests throughout each year to build towards that level.

In addition to there being a whole-school timetable for assessment, there has also been some standardisation of the process. The way that books are marked is now consistent and feedback is given to pupils in the same language, regardless of department. Whilst consistency of approach has been achieved, however, there remains flexibility at department level. Thus, for example, one head of department noted that, whilst she might not assess across every skill area in all tests, she would ensure that all skills were assessed over the course of the year. Her colleague, meanwhile, discussed his department's policy of testing in each of four individual topics over the full course of Key Stage 3, with a final test, combining all four topics, allowing pupils a second chance to demonstrate their skills.

In a more recent development, Newtown has implemented a whole-school focus on 'planning for progression'. Heads of department are now being asked to plan how pupils will progress in particular skill areas, such as use of IT or application of Welsh outside the classroom. It will not be enough to include particular practices in a lesson; each practice must be covered as part of a planned progression from more basic to higher level skills. As one head of department explained, 'we have to think through how we're going to improve ... [pupils'] skills over the course of time, throughout their time at the school'. Although every department must develop its own plan, links between departments will be facilitated by liaison with the designated link coordinator for each skill area. At present, coordinators are carrying out audits of skill levels across the school. Policies will be put in place at Key Stage 3 and then rolled out further up the school.

Rewards
The school has worked to develop a culture that celebrates the success of pupils, both within its walls and in the wider community. 'Good liaison' with the local press has resulted in 'celebration of success being driven in the newspaper publications'. This in turn has helped to transform local perceptions of the school: as one teacher pointed out, 'you can't help but notice the stark contrast' between current results and those of seven years ago.

As well as the annual celebration of pupils' results, senior management have introduced more regular forms of praise. Faculty achievement badges – known as FAB badges – are awarded by heads of department on a half-termly basis. One boy and one girl are selected from each year group in each subject to receive a badge, which recognises pupils who have made a particular effort in a subject. Staff explained that they 'don't give the badge necessarily to the highest level student', but instead reward 'the student who has worked the best. ... If they've put in every bit of effort, they're going to get rewarded.' Two pupils from each year are also rewarded with a £10 WHSmith voucher for overall effort in every lesson.

Although FAB badges are known colloquially among pupils as 'boffin' or 'boff' badges, the evidence suggests that this is an affectionate term. One respondent described how even pupils who 'struggle in all aspects' or who can be 'really wild' will 'wear these badges with pride'. As a parent, she regards such recognition as 'really important'. This view was supported by the pupils themselves, some of whom display all the badges that they have received on the front of their planners.

Rewards for good behaviour are a similar source of motivation for pupils. Clean slate reward days are held once per term for all pupils who have received no more than two detentions in the previous weeks, with those being rewarded allowed to take an early lunch and watch a film in the afternoon. Approximately two thirds of pupils are rewarded in this way each term. Teachers agreed that, from relatively low-key beginnings, the rewards system has grown increasingly successful. One respondent, a Year 10 mentor, explained the current status of clean slates among pupils:

> We've got stickers on the walls ... showing their clean slates and they love it. They're up there checking. These are 14, 15 year old students and you would have thought they wouldn't want [to]. But they like to see that they've got a clean slate going right across.

The clean slate system was particularly singled out by parents as being beneficial for children who are doing well at school and are on target:

> They reward the good behaviour and the good children which is important, because sometimes they can be a little bit forgotten about if they're doing well and they're on track – there doesn't seem the need for them to have an awful lot of attention. But with the rewards ... it's nice that the good children have been rewarded.

Ongoing poor behaviour is dealt with in a variety of ways. Recognising that disruptiveness in the classroom can often stem from pupils spending too long on a single task, one teacher described how he prevents poor behaviour from developing by setting a series of shorter tasks. In a minority of cases, however, pupils are persistently disruptive. Heads of department pay careful attention to the groups in which these children are placed. Wherever possible, to prevent a negative culture from emerging, concentrations of 'lively' pupils are avoided. Pupils can also be moved between classes – sometimes only for a short period of two to three weeks – in an attempt to modify their behaviour using the positive peer pressure of the new class. Where pupils are moved into a higher set, this can also have a motivating effect.

For pupils who have significant problems with their social skills, Newtown has a dedicated behavioural unit. Pupils' main goal during their time in the unit is to improve these skills:

> As opposed to just giving them detentions or removing them from classrooms, there is actually a place to go where they can get positive reinforcement and be taught how to behave.

The school is therefore addressing the root cause of poor behaviour, preventing it from being a persistent barrier to learning. Staff have the data to show what a pupil is capable of and so, as one member of the senior management team put it, 'the smokescreen of a student's behaviour shouldn't stop them succeeding'.

Addressing low attainment
Further dedicated units exist within the school for the provision of targeted and intensive support for pupils with specific needs. The dyslexia unit provides support throughout Key Stages 3 and 4. In the Pontio unit, pupils who have been identified as requiring additional emotional and academic support undergo a phased transition from primary to secondary school. All pupils in the school receive shared lessons in subjects such as design technology, with Pontio unit pupils taught separately in other lessons. This allows them to mix with their peers but also to receive intensive support to bring them up to a suitable level. Pupils in Year 7 with purely curricular needs can be placed in the transition group. Introduced in the current academic year, this class is taught by a single teacher and focuses on developing basic skills. Because she works with them full time and hence knows them extremely well, the teacher is able to tailor her lessons to suit each individual pupil, at the same time as covering required subject content.

Once pupils are established at the school, Newtown's monitoring system allows staff to readily identify those pupils who are at risk either of not reaching the Level 2 threshold at Key Stage 4 or, in some cases, of leaving school with no qualifications at all. Numbers vary by year group, but approximately twenty-five pupils in any year will fall into this category. These pupils receive intensive support to improve their performance. In Years 10 and 11 they are withdrawn each week, as a group, from three of their six timetabled science lessons. This time is used to focus on attainment of key skills qualifications and the Work Skills BTEC. As described below, attention is increasingly turning to the achievement of these qualifications by all pupils at Key Stage 3. However, it is anticipated that a small group of pupils will always require additional support at Key Stage 4.

A limited number of other pupils – who are at some risk but are not in this group – will also be closely monitored, whilst approximately ten pupils per year group will be monitored because of concerns over attendance or challenging home circumstances. Where necessary, individualised plans will be devised for these children. An openness to creating such personalised timetables for pupils was apparent in a number of the interviews conducted at the school.

For all pupils there is a focus on literacy and numeracy across all subjects. Progress has been made on cross-departmental consistency in the use of terminology, as evidenced for instance by the adoption of 'mean', 'median' and 'mode' in place of 'average' by science teachers. In subjects from music to mathematics, attention is paid to explaining the language used at every stage, so that pupils are not prevented from succeeding because of a language barrier. Registration periods and PSE lessons are used to improve skills, through literacy and numeracy groups that pair sixth formers with students lower down the school. Year 7 pupils have recently been involved in reading sessions and learning or refreshing their times tables.

The role of learning support assistants has also been expanded in recent years. As well as providing in-class support for named pupils and the basic skills group, individual LSAs now have responsibilities ranging from assessing reading ages to providing IT key skills support. An increasing number of assistants have obtained or are working towards qualifications including NVQs.

Introducing Level 2 qualifications at KS3
Recognition that a number of Level 2 qualifications also fit the Key Stage 3 curriculum is leading to an important new departure at Newtown. In addition

to receiving an end of key stage level, Year 9 pupils are increasingly working towards achieving a number of Level 2 qualifications, both in 'traditional' subjects and in key skills. The purpose of this is twofold. Firstly, it provides pupils with a clear goal, thus improving motivation. Secondly, it takes pupils some way towards achieving the Level 2 threshold, and hence relieves pressure at Key Stage 4.

The importance of finding new ways to motivate pupils at Key Stage 3 was emphasised by one respondent, who reported that 'our big problem has always been Year 9, because a lot of the pupils know they don't intend carrying on [with this subject] at the end of the year. Trying to keep them focused and trying to keep them going is quite challenging.' One pupil acknowledged that teachers were good at explaining how KS3 subject content could also form part of the required content for later qualifications. However, that the achievement of qualifications is a particularly effective way of addressing demotivation was confirmed by a pupil who contrasted her experience of Years 9 and 10:

> Coming up into Year 10 now, and knowing that your GCSEs are this summer, it really makes you want to work harder and actually get your targets. It is different [at Key Stage 3] because you don't even know what options you're going to take. So if you really hate [a subject] it's just like 'what's the point?' because you'll be dropping it.

The availability since September 2010 of a new BTEC Level 2 qualification in music, the requirements for which are not as great as for the First Certificate in performing arts previously on offer, will allow Newtown pupils to work towards a qualification in parallel with their Key Stage 3 work. The BTEC is attainable at KS3 because there is significant overlap in the work required: pupils already perform as soloists and in ensembles, and undertake research into famous conductors and musicians. In filling their portfolios for end of key stage assessment, they are therefore also producing evidence for the BTEC award. Since the 'vast majority' of pupils will not opt to take music at GCSE, it is hoped that aiming for a qualification will serve to motivate them. For those pupils who attain the qualification, an added incentive is that they will already be 20% of the way towards the Level 2 threshold, before even entering Year 10. This is particularly important for those pupils for whom achieving a significant number of qualifications at Key Stage 4 proves challenging.

For the most able pupils, it is no less important to maintain motivation and challenge. Other departments are therefore planning to offer GCSE qualifications for their highest sets. In modern languages, for example, staff are considering offering a half-GCSE in French. From 2011, the school also hopes to bring in GCSE humanities for the top set in Year 9. This will be delivered through the history, geography and R.E. departments. However, since staff 'don't want to put too much pressure on them', pupils are being consulted before a final decision is made. An additional benefit of engaging with the pupils before introducing the qualification is that 'it makes such a difference asking pupils "what do you want to do?" rather than just telling them "you will be doing this". They suddenly become so much more focused.'

This will build on the success achieved by the Welsh department, which already offers early entry Welsh to its top set. Identified in Year 7, the good Welsh learners know from this point that they will take their GCSE in Year 9. This was identified by the head of department as an important means of giving them focus. Until now this option has only been available to the top set, but the intention is to offer the new, more modular, GCSE to a broader range of pupils. As well as welcoming the focus that studying to GCSE level at Key Stage 3 promotes, pupils can feel the benefit at Key Stage 4. One pupil, who had wanted to take Welsh as a KS4 option, has chosen not to do so because she 'is doing half of the GCSE already in Year 9'. Rather than repeating the work in Year 10, she has been able to take an alternative option, thus 'giving [her] more GCSEs'.

For all pupils, but most particularly for the benefit of those at risk of missing the Level 2 threshold, Newtown has introduced a range of skills qualifications. To date these have largely been completed during Key Stage 4. The school is aiming, however, for increasing numbers of pupils to complete them by the end of Key Stage 3. At present, all pupils have a skills day once per term, during which the timetable is collapsed. KS3 pupils focus on the IT, application of number, communication, problem solving and improving own learning performance key skills.

In Year 10, pupils further develop their problem solving skills and complete accreditation for those skills not completed at Key Stage 3. As well as having dedicated skills days, pupils use PSE lessons throughout Key Stage 4 to complete their portfolios of work. For Year 11 pupils, skills days have been devoted to completion of the Work Skills BTEC. Comprising 40% of the Level 2 threshold for students who complete sufficient units, the BTEC has been introduced to motivate those who are not A*-C candidates and who otherwise 'may have been completely turned off by education'.

The school is currently in a transition phase as it brings forward completion of key skills accreditation from KS4 into KS3. Pupils in Years 9, 10 and 11 are therefore all working towards the same skills. Ultimately, however, it is hoped that the majority of pupils will be 80% of the way towards the Level 2 threshold by the time they begin Year 10. With the pressure to achieve the threshold thus relieved at KS4, the type of pupil who has tended to struggle at GCSE:

> can concentrate on some of the subjects that they're very, very keen on – art, construction, performing arts – which are still big hitters in terms of performance ... but they're keener on them.

Inevitably this will increase the amount of work required at KS3. As a member of the senior management team admitted, 'it's really hard work, for them and for us, because it's ... constant, constant, constant – lots of individualised timetables, lots of staff time being used up, a lot of cajoling and pushing and incentivising to get the students through'. The school's ethos of, and individual teachers' commitment to, not letting students down ensures that, even though some children 'might not thank us for it at the time', that effort is made. Over time, staff are also coming to appreciate the extent to which key skills accreditation can fit on top of existing work, giving a 'rubber stamp' to what they are already doing.

Pupil engagement
Pupils' engagement with Newtown begins with their induction into school life during Year 6. The school holds an open evening, at which pupils can buy their new uniform, and a three day induction during the summer term. Pupils coming to the induction are treated as though they are already Newtown pupils and, very often, 'they just don't want to go back' to primary school again. One parent put her daughter into that category, 'even though [she] loved primary school'. A recent addition to the calendar is an additional day spent at the school in the previous October, during which pupils study practical subjects such as design technology. One respondent noted that 'the feedback that we had from that was really positive. Even though they'd only come for the day and they'd done lots of fun things ... the feeling was for a majority of them that they couldn't wait to come back'.

Contrasting their experiences of primary school with those at Newtown, all of the pupils to whom we spoke agreed that they were now far more engaged in their own learning: 'Here ... you sit by a lot more people and interact with the board and everything', whereas at primary school 'the teacher stood up and taught you and you just had to get on with it'. Whilst this does not necessarily reflect the experience of all primary school pupils, it was clear that Newtown places a particularly strong – and growing – emphasis on listening to pupils' views on a range of issues. Pupils on the School Council described their purpose as being to provide a student viewpoint on issues from teaching methods to wellbeing. One pupil went so far as to compare the Council's role with that of the school's governing body:

> it's like the Council and the governors are the same thing but they're in different positions. So the governors sort out some problems and the Council sort out [the rest].

Pupils' views are currently sought on three principal pedagogic issues: lesson style, subject content and course evaluation.

School Council members listed a number of methods of learning that they find most effective, which they had fed back to the teaching staff. These included:

— learning in groups;
— having the opportunity to communicate with each other as a means of developing understanding;
— actively participating in lessons; and
— being able to have fun while learning, which pupils thought 'works quite well' as a learning aid. Examples of the introduction of 'fun' into lessons included the use of games and of a 'random name generator' in some lessons to determine which pupil would answer the next question.

In terms of subject content, teachers explained how they were increasingly giving their pupils 'a definite input ... into the curriculum'. This includes both 'what we do and how we do it'. One example given was the history department's recent decision to canvas pupils' views on what to learn about in their World War One module. Alongside core content, pupils will now be taught about areas of particular interest to them. One pupil described how this would include focusing on the use of machinery, war poetry and the roles played by women. This was good, she said, because 'I quite like learning about something I want to learn about'.

Some departments also invite pupils to evaluate their units at the end of each year. Several heads of department detailed how pupils are asked which units they do and do not enjoy, why this is and what improvements they think could be made. Although the prospect of inviting evaluation can be daunting in the beginning, teachers felt that pupils are 'honest' but also 'fair'. They also recognised the benefit for them and for their pupils:

> I'd rather know, at the end of the day. If I'm not doing something in a way which makes sense to them, then I need to know how I can change it so that it does make sense to them, and so that it doesn't cause me problems down the line...

It was apparent from pupils' own comments that they value the opportunities to engage that are afforded to them. Moreover, their enthusiasm for being able to learn some content that they had chosen, in a way that engages their sense of enjoyment, mirrors one teacher's observation that pupils become 'so much more focused' when included in this way. Staff expressed a commitment to listen more to children in the future. This, together with curricular innovations at Key Stage 3 aimed at motivating pupils from across the ability spectrum, encapsulates the two goals that recurred throughout the interviews: an absolute determination to secure the best for, and from, each pupil and, to that end, an ongoing focus on finding the methods that will best achieve this.

Chapter 8

St Joseph's R.C. High School

School performance at KS3

St Joseph's R.C. High School consistently achieves a high level of performance at Key Stage 3. The contextual value added scores in two of the three years 2006-2008 have a statistically significant positive value, demonstrating that St Joseph's pupils perform better than is expected given performance on intake. In 2006, the proportion of pupils achieving Level 5 or above in Newport schools was broadly the same as the all-Wales average. The St Joseph's figures were fourteen percentage points higher in English, eleven points higher in mathematics and seven points higher in science[23].

This high level of attainment continues at Key Stage 4. The proportion of pupils in 2006 who achieved the core subject indicator – grades A*-C in each of mathematics, science and English or Welsh – was, at 42%, broadly commensurate with the local authority (39%) and all-Wales (41%) averages. However, the proportion of pupils achieving five or more grades A*-C in any subjects was five percentage points higher than the Welsh average and ten points higher than the local authority average. The number of pupils attaining at least five grades A*-G was also well above average[24].

Combined with a 2007 Estyn inspection report that awarded a top grade in each of the seven key questions, these results show St Joseph's to be an extremely high performing school. The headteacher argues that:

> ...why we've been reasonably successful at Key Stage 3, and likewise throughout the school's journey into Key Stage 4 and 5, is because we've known the value of Key Stage 3. I've always stressed that it's a building block of education, a very critical

---

23 St Joseph's R.C. High School, Prospectus 2007.

24 Estyn, 2007, A Report on the Quality of Secondary Education in St Joseph's RC High School.

building block. So with our staffing, when we're actually timetabling staff we ensure that we've got some key players teaching in Key Stage 3.

Whilst the school's self-evaluation exactly matched the Estyn grades, suggesting that the management is well aware of the school's strengths, the headteacher clearly did not regard the school as being able to rest on its laurels, describing the Key Stage 3 figures as 'look[ing] *quite* strong' and the school as being '*reasonably* successful' (emphasis added). That there is a culture of innovation and improvement, and a desire to improve attainment, within the school became apparent throughout the course of our interviews.

School culture
The school's ethos foregrounds inclusion – as evidenced by the term's adoption four years ago by the then special needs, now inclusion, department – and ongoing engagement of parents, staff and pupils. The school aims to engage parents and carers in their children's learning wherever it can, and was described as 'very lucky in the way that we can get parents and carers in, because what the child experiences outside of the school we feel is important'. Information on their children's progress is shared with all parents at various stages during the school year. It is not unheard of for the school to have 95% attendance at parents' evenings, partly as a result of the school's efforts to engage some of the most hard to reach parents. Parental attendance at parents' evenings is tracked, allowing staff to determine where additional effort will be required to establish and maintain contact.

The school works closely with other agencies, including Newport's Preventative Services Group. This group has a representative working with Newport's Catholic schools cluster who is able to visit families and work with them outside the school setting, facilitating access to a range of support services as required. This can include, for example, family intervention programmes for parenting and caring. Whilst it can be 'tricky' to engage parents, according to the headteacher:

> we push it from the first time I meet the parents. You know, we're in this together. And if you work with us we'll try and do the very best for your child, but it'll be much better if you help as well. The three of us – the child, the family and the school – working will have a better impact than just us trying to do it on our own.

This ethos of joint effort is complemented by an attention to promoting an enthusiasm for learning. The headteacher argued that:

> if we get [Key Stage 3] right, if we get them attending, loving learning, ... [if we] stretch them whatever their levels are, and [if we get] the right interventions in school, if we get it right, when they come through to Key Stage 4 they're going to fly a little bit more.

Expanding on this theme, she explained that, at the same time as focusing on the quality of the learning and continuing to ask how children are progressing:

> there's got to be some fun in learning as well. I think we've gone too serious in schools. And I think the new skills curriculum is opening up staff to be creative again and give the children a bit of fun.

The importance of this approach was underscored by one of the teachers interviewed, who compared St Joseph's with previous schools in which he had taught:

> In the two previous schools I've been in, where I've found teachers have been struggling, and where pupils are certainly not motivated, I think it's where teachers feel that they have to be straight-jacketed.

Whilst teachers are allowed the space at St Joseph's to innovate in the classroom, as detailed below, the school also makes sure that 'the CPD for staff is appropriate' and that 'we share good practice within and across the school'. There are, for instance, 'professional learning communities' within the school which identify and share good practice, and encourage staff to 'talk and be reflective' about what they are doing. In a formal sense these communities are a recent development, although for a number of years the school has held a Learning Forum. This after school meeting provides teachers with a platform to discuss new developments that they have implemented, and it was as a result of one such meeting that Philosophy for Children – an approach discussed in greater detail below – was rolled out across the school from its starting point in the English department. Importantly, the headteacher's assertion that 'there's quite a sense of being engaged in learning ourselves' finds support in the views of a large number of the interviewed staff, who detailed a range of ways in which support is provided for their continuing professional development.

Examples were given of how good practice is shared in relation to quite specific themes. Each of the core subjects has a communication champion, whose responsibility it is to disseminate the latest thinking on developing pupils' communication skills from the school's communication coordinator to his or her department. Other working parties exist to formulate policy on behaviour and thinking skills development at the whole-school level. In addition to these formal mechanisms, teachers are encouraged to exchange ideas informally: in the history department, for instance, teachers not only talk over lunch and at the start of the school day but also use a shared area on the computer network to disseminate resources.

Observation of lessons in all key stages is being used as a further opportunity to share good practice. The culture at St Joseph's was described by members of the senior management team as one of self-review by departments. Any member of a department can initiate a review, the focus of which can be any element of teaching practice, which is then led by the head of department. The greater number of lesson observations is undertaken by teaching staff, rather than management, and when members of the SMT do observe lessons this tends to follow an invitation to do so from the department. Following observation of classroom practice, a report is compiled by the head of department. The role of the SMT was characterised by respondents as being to support middle management in undertaking these reviews, principally through provision of relevant training, and to facilitate the sharing of good practice identified within departments across the school.

One positive factor highlighted by several respondents was the use of external speakers and advisers to introduce new concepts and methods to the school. The school has, for example, implemented a cross-curricular project for pupils which runs for several days during the summer term; topics covered have included an Olympics project, the scheme of work for which was produced by the then science adviser to the Newport schools. The use of 'brilliant speakers' at Inset days was also mentioned, with a recent presentation by Paul Ginnis, a former teacher and now education adviser, on effective learning being singled out.

The school also supports staff who wish to continue their professional development through externally run courses. The headteacher noted that she has 'got a number of staff doing Masters [degrees] and on the iNet Developing Leaders course and doing action research in the school'. Staff have to complete these courses part-time during their evenings, 'so it's pretty tough on them', but funding is available towards their fees. This support extends beyond teaching staff to support staff as well. One learning support assistant described how the school had supported her through university, paying 50% of her MA course fee, and how this had a beneficial impact on the pupils:

> They are pushing people to go and develop themselves, and I think when you do that then obviously what's being passed on to the children is more up to date.

The school's head of inclusion also noted the importance of having 'very highly skilled' support assistants, arguing that 'they're skilled at what they do, they know what they're doing and they bring something that we can't, and that's key'. They have all done a lot of training and 'are always moving on in their own CPD, none of them are stagnating'. In the words of one support assistant, who is also a parent governor at the school, the result is that 'everybody is getting what they need, from the children up to the staff'.

Pupil engagement

Pupil voice – the engagement of children in the life of school and in their own learning – is an important focus at St Joseph's. As the headteacher said, 'it's their school'. Critically, pupil voice is not simply about 'uniform, toilets and food, or buses – we've been there, done that – but it's about what they like in lessons'. The school recently conducted an oracy review in which children were asked what they like in lessons. The results of this were turned into a display, so that pupils could see that their views were having an impact. A similar survey of attitudes to the use of technology has also been carried out. These initiatives are headed up by the deputy head, demonstrating the importance assigned to pupil voice.

In talking to other members of the senior management team and to pupils, the range of opportunities for pupils to discuss their views on teaching and learning became apparent. In addition to one-off occasions on which pupils' opinions are sought, the school now has a nutrition action group and a school council that discusses pedagogic issues. In a more creative development, on the day of our visit to the school SJTV, the school's new television station, was launched; this too was billed as 'a vehicle for pupils' voice'. The school's assistant headteacher in charge of KS3 told us that:

> I think we're trying to involve students at every level. If we have a review of anything we're always trying to talk to children and get their views as well as their ideas. I think that's just become a part... it's really becoming embedded now into what we do.

She concluded that 'the important thing is that they actually see some change as a result of that. They get some feedback, so you've got this is what you've said to us and this is what we're doing'. Her colleague added that this is part of trying to build confidence in pupils that 'they have something worth saying and we want to listen to them, we want to hear what they're saying'.

This confidence was apparent in the pupils interviewed, who also confirmed the range of opportunities available for sharing their opinions. They reported that opportunities were provided in personal and social education (PSE) lessons to talk about the types of teaching that they enjoy, and that further occasions to share their views came from requests to meet with the school governors. In addition to discussing oracy with them, pupils had been questioned about the science curriculum. One pupil who had spoken to the governors reflected that:

> I think they listened quite well, and they were interested to know what we thought about these new science themes and how everything worked and the change to the curriculum.

A measure of how embedded pupil engagement is within the school is that it extends beyond these instances and into the classroom. Pupils are encouraged to reflect on their own learning. As a parent governor described it, 'children are given time to think, to digest, and they're encouraged to ask questions... The children [are] taking the reins, the teachers are guiding them.'

Curricular innovations

This approach is underpinned by the principles of Assessment for Learning and Philosophy for Children (P4C), both of which are employed across the school. The purpose of Philosophy for Children is to encourage pupils to reflect and talk more within lessons, moving the teacher to the role of a facilitator who guides the pupils towards a deeper understanding of themes and concepts. In a P4C lesson, the entire lesson is devoted to a 'community of enquiry', in which pupils think about and discuss a single theme. Typically, St Joseph's pupils will be shown a stimulus, which might include poems, a song or images, that relates to the theme under discussion. The pupils then formulate a question about what they have seen and spend the remainder of the lesson answering that question.

According to the teacher responsible for introducing it to St Joseph's, Philosophy for Children is 'massive' in primary schools and, whilst not as embedded in Newport as in Swansea, where the use of a dedicated Philosophy for Children teacher has been trialled, its use is growing. Whereas secondary schools 'tend to be known ... for being more traditional and not being so open to opinions and things like that', pupils are used in primary school to an environment in which 'they sit and share and talk'. The continuation of this more discursive style of lesson into secondary school is thus regarded as a positive step. Improved outcomes have already been observed. Whilst the focus of these lessons is on oracy, this teacher has noticed 'a huge improvement in [pupils'] written work... If their oral communication improves then it tends to be that so does the writing'.

Two additional oracy targets are being used across the school. To encourage participation the first method is the 'no hands up' principle, whereby the teacher asks a question, allows pupils time to think about the answer and then randomly selects one to answer. The second approach is to reduce teacher talk during lessons to no more than seven minutes. This came about in response to the visit by Paul Ginnis, who discussed the idea of pupil-centred lessons. This fits well with the school's existing commitment to oracy and thus, although reduced teacher talk is 'quite difficult at times', it remains a focus. In the English department, 'the majority of our lessons are [now] speaking and listening centred but with reading and writing outcomes'.

Pupils welcomed this approach to learning:

> In geography [the teacher] doesn't really talk a lot. He just says something and you get on with it really. [Year 8 pupil]

> The teachers communicate well with the students... They all get on with us. They don't completely take charge, they let you be independent, do your own little projects and teach each other. But

then they don't give you too much freedom so that you just don't learn anything. [Year 9 pupil]

Other subjects have also introduced a range of new methods and technologies to the classroom. Many of these developments can be seen to stem from the adoption of a combination of a skills-based curriculum and Assessment for Learning, the process of engaging pupils in understanding where they are in their learning and what they need to do to progress. A focus in PSE lessons on the Improving Own Learning and Performance key skill serves to reinforce Assessment for Learning techniques, which are embedded not only in the core subjects but across the whole curriculum.

In P.E. lessons, for example, each child has a record card on which the four areas of the curriculum relating to physical education are listed. The child enters a smiley, unsure or unhappy face according to whether she is confident in each area, from which she can determine a target for the term. The National Curriculum levels have also been rewritten in terminology to which pupils can better relate, and notice boards are being placed in the school's sports areas which will carry key words that they can adopt in setting their targets. Whilst the focus of each lesson is on getting the pupils active, key skills such as problem-solving, working with others and communication are an integral part of this, and teachers also encourage pupils to make connections with skills used in other subjects. As the head of department made clear, 'if [P.E. teachers] are not putting skills into their lessons, then they're not really encouraging the whole development [of the pupil]'.

In art, the emphasis has been shifted to allowing pupils to experience a range of artistic processes. Programs like Photoshop are now used, in a departure from the limited focus on watercolours and pencils that was originally in place. The head of department contrasted this variety with 'lots of schools [where] they have quite a long project':

> Purposefully I've kept it very short, so there's short spells and then you move, so that they don't get fed up with the same sort of work.

She attributed the increase in the number of pupils achieving Level 5 or above at KS3, currently 91% of pupils, to the use of a range of processes and the short projects. Internal competitions run by the department and entry of pupils' work into external competitions are a motivating factor, and examples of pupils' work form a constantly changing display around the department. The department has also designed its schemes of work far more creatively, and booklets containing photographs of pupils' work at different levels are referred to far more often than the written schemes. The impact of this renewed creativity is apparent in the numbers of pupils opting to take GCSE Art: after one year of the new system, numbers jumped from approximately 24 to 84. These pupils have now reached A Level, where numbers have similarly risen, from two or three to 25.

The impact of the skills-based curriculum is apparent in core subjects such as science, where it has resulted in 'a huge shift' over the past few years. The emphasis is now on teaching skills *through* scientific knowledge. As one respondent put it, whilst 'the scientific part is still important [and] we still like to make good scientists, I think good learners bring about good scientists'. A shift to the use of themes – of which Crime Scene Investigation is a popular example used by this school – has been central to the stimulation of pupils' interest, and has also allowed the science department to collaborate more closely with other departments; whilst the English department might focus on writing up a related court case, the science and mathematics departments work together on equations and the use of calculators.

The reintroduction of an element of 'fun' into learning, the need for which was highlighted by the headteacher, is not only achieved through the use of cross-cutting themes, but also through the introduction of a broader range of teaching methods and technologies. Consistent with the Philosophy for Children approach, pupils are encouraged to give presentations to classmates more often – a positive feature mentioned by one of the pupils interviewed – and to use a range of media during lessons. In mathematics, for example, pupils are exposed to resources from the Internet, including from the Association of Teachers of Mathematics, make frequent use of personal whiteboards for sharing answers, and interact using overhead projectors. This use of multiple methods and technologies, with frequent shifts to new topics, was a recurrent feature in each of the six subjects for which interviews were conducted.

Reflecting on the school's approach, the headteacher noted that 'from outside looking in, I suppose we're quite traditional in the fact that we're teaching subject areas'. It is clear, however, that the methods employed in the classroom have evolved substantially in recent years, in large part in response to opportunities afforded by the skills-based curriculum. The use of Philosophy for Children is a significant new departure, one which was contrasted by one respondent with the 'more traditional' approach most often associated with secondary education. Together with the universal embedding of Assessment for Learning techniques in lessons and the focus on communication skills, this is regarded as 'critical' to moving pupils forward at Key Stage 3.

In addition, the school is in the first year of a trial of humanities lessons, in which Year 7 pupils receive five lessons per fortnight of humanities rather than three lessons each of geography and history. Reservations raised included the loss of one lesson per fortnight and, given that each class will have one teacher, either a history or geography specialist, the impact on assessment in the area outside the teacher's specialism. It was also suggested that 'perhaps we're sending out the message that history and geography are not as important by doing this'. These concerns notwithstanding, the senior management team 'may roll out' this programme. As they were keen to point out, they do not make significant changes such as this without careful thought; this development has been undertaken in a 'controlled' manner as a means of aiding the teaching of skills, and will be reviewed to ensure that its impact is positive. Members of the SMT also emphasised that they have full confidence in the ability of staff to maintain high standards, and that the transition to humanities lessons would not have occurred had this not been the case.

Motivation and challenge
One teacher to whom we spoke acknowledged that:

> even though we do get very good results at Key Stage 3, I think we do still have the Key Stage 3 dip [in that] some pupils will come in on a Level 5 in English ... and they will leave with a 5 ... in Year 9. [As long as] they've still got the 5 then that won't be considered [a problem] because as long as they've got the 5 it's fine. It doesn't matter if they came in with it in Year 7.

She also made it clear, however, that underachievement is something that her department aims to pick up on. In the English department a higher proportion of boys than girls falls into this category. The focus on oracy introduced by Philosophy for Children has had a beneficial impact on this group, 'because boys tend to like to talk about things rather than write about them'. A new intervention programme is also being started with Year 9: any boy who has not moved level since Year 7 will have specific work undertaken with them.

Key Skills Communication Level 2 is also being introduced for all Year 9 pupils as a bridge between Key Stages 3 and 4. As a unit 'normally done in the sixth form', it was described as 'quite difficult' for KS3 pupils, but was regarded as beneficial 'because it keeps them really, really focused for the end of Year 9, because that's the time when behaviour can slip'. The two top sets will be challenged still further by being entered at Level 3.

A similar focus on trajectory as well as absolute standard was also discussed by other teachers. In science, the removal of SATs tests was described as having led to a certain loss of drive among pupils. Motivating pupils has been a challenge, but the introduction of themes has been 'a big thing that we have done to try to stimulate pupils'. Because pupils 'don't feel like they're doing work' there has been an observed increase in their motivation levels.

As in English, the science department has, over the past three years, paid increasing attention to gifted and talented pupils. Until this focus was implemented there were 'quite a large number who were just sitting around'. To combat this the department has introduced more open-ended tasks, which incorporate a range of key skills and a larger element of prose writing. Greater attention has also been paid to differentiation within lessons, using worksheets at different levels, to ensure that each pupil is pushed as far as possible. Additional worksheets have also been introduced in the art department. Once every two or three weeks, Year 9 pupils who are registered as gifted and talented are given an extra task which they complete in a dedicated workbook.

Literacy and numeracy
Support for gifted and talented pupils is also now provided as part of the school's literacy support. Three groups of pupils are targeted for support. These are pupils with a spelling age of seven or eight on entry to St Joseph's, pupils operating at Level 4 on entry who have been identified as capable of achieving a higher level, and the most able pupils in the year group.

The first group includes pupils identified during Year 6 as having a spelling age of seven or eight. This amounts to approximately 24 pupils. Withdrawal from lessons is limited to once per week, to limit disruption to lessons, during which time small groups of three pupils receive additional support. For the remainder of these pupils' time, resources and lesson plans are provided by the leader of the literacy intervention programmes for completion in lessons.

The second group of targeted pupils comprises all those with a Level 4 on entry and whose teachers indicate that they should be performing better. These pupils are subject to an intensive programme of withdrawal. Following selection in the autumn term, support is provided between January and Easter to around thirty pupils. A rolling timetable during this time limits the impact on individual subjects. The prime objectives for these pupils are to increase confidence and to raise attainment to Level 5.

Finally, support is given to the most able and talented pupils, who might otherwise 'cruise' and thus fail to achieve their full potential. In 2009, the 30 most able Year 7 pupils were withdrawn from one English lesson per week following their examinations in the summer term. Texts covered by this group included Ibsen's Doll's House and the poetry of Blake, and themes including the conflict between nature and technology and the portrayal of females in fiction were addressed. A similar programme for Year 8 pupils runs from Easter until shortly before the summer examination period. Analysis of poetry, novels and plays is combined with discussion of works of art.

Each of these programmes is organised by the leader of the literacy intervention programmes, one of three learning support assistants assigned to the core departments of English, mathematics and science. The English department's LSA works with the literacy coordinator – who is also second in department – and the head of inclusion to set and implement policy, with a further ten LSAs helping to deliver the resultant strategies.

The support assistant in charge of numeracy catch-up programmes, a former teacher who has been in post for a year, has a somewhat different role from the English LSA. The position, part-funded by the Newport Advisory Service, was created a number of years ago to allow the provision of a numeracy acceleration programme. Additional numeracy support throughout the school is provided by another member of staff who is the designated numeracy coordinator. If the opportunity arises, this is work with which the LSA would like to become involved. At present, the numeracy acceleration programme targets Year 7 pupils with a high Level 3 to low Level 4. Thirty-six pupils received support in the last academic year, through rolling withdrawal from lessons.

Reading Buddy and Number Buddy programmes also operate during the year. Year 7 and 8 pupils are paired with Year 12s, with support from the literacy and numeracy teams and the school librarian. Reading Buddies begins in the autumn term, with a ten week Number Buddies programme for Level 2 and 3 pupils following on in the second term. For those pupils requiring additional reading support, a small Reading Buddies course then takes place in the summer term, run by the librarian and an LSA in form time. Although 'it's a phenomenal amount of work to do', the English department's LSA argued that 'if you do it, I think you do see overall a real benefit... I feel [we're] always moving forward, I feel positive about it, the whole drive is positive', a view echoed by his numeracy counterpart.

Mixed ability teaching

On entry in Year 7, pupils receive the vast majority of their teaching in mixed ability classes. This is regarded as central to ensuring that all pupils are brought on to their full ability. This approach means that the school does not have special needs classes, which is welcomed by the head of inclusion:

> The big thing that we've done here is inclusive practices in the classroom. So we don't have a special needs class... I can't understand myself the concept of a special needs class. It doesn't for me make any intellectual sense because ... a special needs class for me [involves] putting the most extremes in one place and expecting a member of staff to cope with them.

The school has moved towards this state over a number of years and there has been 'a lot of training and work – and there's more to be done – with staff about good practice for a mixed ability class. And it ain't as hard as you might think. You know, we've looked at very simple things like the structure of the lesson, like a good plenary, like good starters. Differentiation is the most difficult thing, it's the biggest challenge, but that's the way forward here'.

With progression through the school, pupils are exposed to a range of setting practices in different subjects, although 'at no point ... will a child be set for every subject'. Rationales for setting include, in mathematics – which sets from Year 7 – the fact that able and talented pupils can be pushed without intimidating those with a lower ability or low confidence. P.E. also sets from Year 7. When combined with a rotation to a new sport every six weeks, this has led to a marked increase in participation. A particular benefit has been that it has allowed teachers to focus on different skills with each set, thus ensuring that the less athletic are also stretched, on tasks such as coaching.

By contrast, the history department has moved away from strict sets. Mixed ability in Years 7 and 8 gives way to a division between two top sets and six mixed ability classes in Year 9, before a return to mixed ability at GCSE. Bottom sets could be extremely hard work for teachers, not least because 'the children get the message that they are lower ability [and] they can switch off'. The aim now is to 'try to pull the bottom end up' through exposure to more able pupils.

When asked about their preferences, one Year 9 pupil explained that being in sets 'is easier, because whatever set you're in is your ability to do stuff, so everyone in your set is at the same [point]'. By contrast, in Year 7, 'because we're all doing the same work, if someone struggles then the teacher has to stop the lesson to help them, and then the people that are a higher ability then get slowed down in their work'. Echoing the mathematics department's rationale for setting, another pupil pointed out that 'sometimes, if everyone else gets what you're doing and you don't it could be a bit embarrassing to ask, because you might not want to make a fool of yourself'. By Year 9, however, this was regarded as being less of a problem because 'we're all friends now and we know each other, so we really don't care'.

Data use: transition and monitoring

St Joseph's gathers as much data as possible on the academic status and well-being of pupils from its partner primaries prior to their arrival in Year 7. According to the headteacher, knowing the children very well before they arrive and working with the primaries prior to their arrival to smooth the transition has had a most positive impact on KS3 performance. The use of bridging units and of the same vocabulary in secondary as in primary school has led to a consistency in approach across all schools. A number of teachers emphasised the importance of moderation work over the past decade to ensure that levels are consistently applied by all parties. This approach was described by one teacher as a 'spiralling up of the curriculum, so we're actually carrying on [from primary school teaching]'.

One particularly significant impact of a close relationship with the partner primaries has been an improved awareness at St Joseph's of how advanced pupils in Year 6 already are. The deputy headteacher explained how, in her own department, 'the whole structure of our schemes of work changed dramatically' to present greater challenge from the outset to Year 7 pupils. This had included looking at the texts offered, at the reading and writing activities and at developing communication. Another member of the senior management team expressed her concern that Year 7 pupils are often seen as the 'babies', whereas at primary level they have been used to being the most senior pupils:

> I make sure that as far as possible every NQT [newly qualified teacher] goes into a primary school and does some work with Year 6 ... to see what they've achieved. ... So that they're not feeding them too much, they're not treating them as little babies, that they see them achieving what they are at the top end of the primary sector, so that we can move them on. I think that's important.

Once the pupils reach St Joseph's, the data held on them are collated using the Serco information system. This includes records of attendance, behaviour, timetables, test marks, reports and targets. This system is available to all teachers, but the school tries 'not to swamp them with lots of data because some staff can't see through the data'. Information is therefore shared in a targeted way, supported by the school's dedicated data manager.

Additional tracking is performed at the department level, with termly or end of unit tests providing an indication of pupil progress. Heads of department monitor achievement and, where necessary, refer pupils for one or more of the additional support services described above. Heads of year also provide an important overview, and meet with form tutors every morning to discuss any matters arising in relation to either achievement or behaviour.

The systems in place for monitoring performance and addressing weaknesses are clearly vital in creating a consistent approach at the whole-school level. Moreover, day-to-day engagement of the senior management team with teaching staff was clearly valued when it occurred. Formal 'learning walks' and informal visits to lessons, during both of which senior managers are able to gain an overview of activity within the school whilst raising their own profile with pupils, were both mentioned as valuable. Two benefits of this role being taken on by senior management were highlighted by one teacher: it is important in preventing heads of year from becoming 'snowed under' with additional responsibilities; and the presence of the SMT can serve to reinforce good behaviour in the classroom.

It is clear, however, that the dedicated teaching staff have the most direct role in creating positive outcomes. Staff were variously described as 'particularly hard working' and 'quality', 'mak[ing] themselves available, it doesn't matter if it's a break time or lunchtime, they are there', and 'working as a team'. Much of this came through most clearly from the teachers themselves during our interviews with them. From their enthusiasm for their subject and from the volume and range of materials that they brought with them, unprompted, to discuss, their commitment to what one described as 'the constant work in progress' of developing their teaching was obvious.

Chapter 9:
Ysgol David Hughes

School performance at KS3

At its most recent inspection, in 2006, Ysgol David Hughes was deemed to be 'a very good school with many outstanding features'[25]. According to the Key Stage 3 contextual value added data for the three years 2006-2008, the school did not add value at a statistically significant level. However, as the school points out, based on 2010 simple value added scores it *is* adding value at KS3 and is in the second quartile of schools for all key subjects except science, for which it is in the first quartile.

In absolute terms the school produces Key Stage 3 results that are higher than both national and local authority averages. In 2009, 77% of pupils achieved Level 5 or above in Welsh, 76% in English, 78% in mathematics and 88% in science. In total, 69% of pupils achieved the core subject indicator[26]. Equivalent scores for Wales as a whole were 75% in Welsh, 71% in English, 74% in mathematics and 76% in science. 61% of pupils across Wales and 62% on Anglesey achieved the core subject indicator[27].

This high standard is maintained throughout Years 10 and 11, culminating in GCSE results well above the local authority and national averages. The proportion of pupils achieving grades A*-C in English, mathematics and science is between ten and fourteen points higher than these averages. In Welsh, the proportion of A*-C passes is seven percentage points higher than the local authority average and a full 26% higher than the all-Wales average[28].

---

25   Estyn, 2006, Inspection under Section 10 of the School Inspections Act 1996, Ysgol David Hughes.

26   Ysgol David Hughes, 2010, School Development Plan.

27   www.statswales.wales.gov.uk, Schools and Teachers, Examinations and Assessments, Key Stage 3, Key Stage 3 results by subject.

28   Ysgol David Hughes, September 2010, School Handbook.

In spite of these results, and perhaps in tacit recognition that there is room for the school to add further value at Key Stage 3, senior management acknowledge that:

> we're a school that's doing well. ... We're getting progress, it's always improving as such, but actually maybe the speed of improvement isn't where we want it to be. We want to see more pupils achieving more Level 5s, we want to see the pupils following that on and getting the Level 2 threshold.

Management and leadership
This drive for yet further improvement is underpinned by the school's ethos. As described by a member of the senior management team:

> it's all about where pupils are going to go next, really. I think morally we have an absolute duty to make sure that pupils get their basics, and they get their maths, their English, their science, their Welsh... they get the core subject indicator, make sure that their skills are improving, and they get the experiences in the range of different subjects, so that they can come back to school if they want to come back to the sixth form and do their A Levels, or they could go on to an apprenticeship, or they could go on to college. The bottom line is that we're empowering them to make what they actually want ... out of their own lives.

In achieving this end, the importance of experimentation with new teaching methods was apparent. A number of teachers discussed how they are encouraged 'to be bold and be prepared to experiment'. Specific examples of this experimentation are detailed below. Teachers and management stressed that critical to the success of this culture of enquiry into new methods is the strong leadership exhibited by the management team.

The teachers and learning assistants interviewed characterised the senior management team's approach as an 'open door' policy. This was explained as consisting of an openness to negotiation, on factors ranging from budgets to teaching methods, and active encouragement of contributions from all staff in meetings:

> Obviously [it's] very much a case [that] we listen to the

information that's presented to us, but we are always encouraged to respond.

The headteacher in particular was mentioned for his trust of staff and his openness to 'challenge'. One respondent noted that she 'can knock on Dr Jones' door any time and he's very supportive, and any help that he can give he will give'. The school was also described, however, as being 'very lucky' in terms of its middle managers who, because of their interest in developments in the education field, are well placed to capitalise on the freedom given to them to experiment with new approaches.

The practical upshot of this policy, described as a 'great positive' that one teacher 'couldn't emphasise enough', is that it has created what two respondents termed a 'happy' working environment. Expanding on this theme, a third said:

> You have conversations with people and it's so exhilarating. ...
> You've got people you can bounce ideas [off]. They come to you:
> "what do you think of this?". And that's great, it's really good. This
> isn't something that's new to this school.

Thus when teachers wish to explore new approaches, with a view to implementing them in their classes, they can feel 'happy and comfortable' that 'something will be sorted out' to provide them with whatever support they need.

The role of the local authority

Further to support provided through the sharing of information within the school, an important source of advice – mentioned on numerous occasions during our visit – was the local education authority's advisory service Cynnal. Cynnal provides three types of curricular support to all schools in the authority:

— training and support for curricular and management developments;
— in-service training; and
— management training and support.

Cynnal has a service level agreement which specifies the support that each secondary school will receive[29]. In relation to curricular and management support each school is entitled to the following:

— a total of six days' advisory time from Cynnal subject advisors, to be spread between individual subjects and cross-curricular matters such as assessment and self-evaluation, for the purpose of sharing curricular priorities with the school and responding to the school's own needs;
— four half-day visits to address the school's own curricular development priorities;
— up to 8 days of advisory support for schools undergoing inspection;
— two half-day visits to support newly qualified teachers;
— additional telephone and email advice on national and local curricular developments and on candidates for teaching posts;
— at the school's request, an advisor will visit the school to support any teacher experiencing specific difficulties, will identify needs and priorities, and will draw up an action plan;
— advice is also given at the catchment-area level on primary-secondary school links.

Cynnal also draws up and delivers in-service training based on national and local priorities and developments. For school management, it coordinates communication structures between senior management in the area's schools and hosts an annual conference for headteachers.

Respondents reported there to be excellent links with the advisors. In one senior manager's words, 'they are there to work with us, and they're very flexible'. Thus, for example, the head of geography, who has recently returned from maternity leave, was meeting with an advisor on the afternoon of our visit to discuss strategies for reflection. Although the advisor in question was a specialist in English who was visiting the English department in the morning, she was happy to stay to speak to the head of geography. Whenever individuals want to develop a particular strategy, 'there's that kind of relationship' that they can approach Cynnal for advice.

The LEA advisors provide 'a lot of input' which, because it comes from outside Ysgol David Hughes, increases confidence that the school is up to date with current thinking. In addition to Cynnal providing this overview to the school, both parties are engaged in developing a range of specific initiatives. Several of these are detailed below.

---

29   Cynnal, 2009/2012 Service Level Agreement (Secondary).

— One of the teachers in the school's catchment area has been undertaking work for Cynnal on the moderation of Year 6 levels in Welsh, and the school has been part of the WJEC's moderation pilot project. The English department has also been undertaking similar moderation work, which will put Ysgol David Hughes in a positive position as and when nationwide moderation is rolled out.

— The Cynnal science advisor has been working with every catchment area in Anglesey and Gwynedd to develop a more consistent understanding of levels between all primary and secondary schools. The science department has also opened discussions with the advisor about the possibility of developing a science bridging project between Years 6 and 7.

— Literacy is being developed across the school through the development by each department of one extended writing task to be set per term for each year group. Guidelines are being created to help departments define the grammar and answer structure that they will be looking for.

— Cynnal is also working with the school to investigate how best to spend money allocated for special educational needs support. They are currently analysing the results obtained under the initiatives employed, and will be helping the school to assess where to allocate money in the future, in the context of limited resources.

This dedicated and coordinated input from the local authority is not something that was apparent in the other schools visited. It is clear not only that this system has been an important catalyst for change in recent years but also, from the responses of teachers and management at Ysgol David Hughes, that it is viewed in an overwhelmingly positive light.

Pupil engagement
In addition to learning from external sources:

> it's an important feature of the school that [pupils] have the opportunity to express their opinion. Hopefully we do a lot of that, we do listen... We're trying to raise the profile of the School Council as well now. The work that they do is much more

impressive than it was in the last few years.

Pupils' opinions have, for instance, been sought on Assessment for Learning techniques, whilst their insights on the importance of form tutors to raising their academic performance have led directly to the introduction of extended tutorial times. Feedback from Year 7s on their first days and weeks at the school will also be used to improve the induction programme in future years. The pupils interviewed agreed that they had been asked to give feedback on various issues, but 'not a lot'. However, although they appeared not to have given formal feedback on many occasions, their responses suggested that they are closely involved in day-to-day engagement with their own learning.

The first of the two ways in which this manifests itself is through the school's use of Assessment for Learning principles. Assessment for Learning 'has become quite well established across departments', following a focus on it in the school's self-evaluation in three of the past four years. A working group has been set up to maintain this focus, with good practice also shared among teachers. A balance was sought between external advice and sharing of 'in-house' developments, because the school wanted to ensure that this approach was not regarded as new, but rather as a formalisation of existing good practice.

An initial emphasis on the learner has given way in the past year to a focus on both the learner and the teacher. This grew out of a recognition that pupils can only determine their own success criteria if they are given the opportunity to do so. Thus the notion of the teacher as facilitator has come to the fore. The three areas to which particular attention has been paid are staff assessment and peer assessment of progress, and the sharing of learning objectives in lessons.

Recognising that these are not new initiatives to be introduced wholesale has allowed individual departments to adopt their own techniques. In the English department, for example, a learning criteria pyramid is displayed at the beginning of every module, showing the *foundation* that all pupils must achieve in terms of spelling, punctuation and grammar, followed by what they *should* and *could* attempt, and topped off by what they might *aim* to achieve. Pupils are encouraged to evaluate their own performance and maintain a log that enables them to keep targets and teacher comments to the fore.

As part of the school-wide commitment to trying new approaches in the classroom, teachers have also experimented with 'no hands up'. The verdict on this was that 'we've not got there, we've not cracked it', and lessons have moved instead towards a greater focus on using initiatives including talking partners and 'think, pair, share' as means of ensuring that every pupil is engaged. The foundation to all of these initiatives is now the Learning to Learn module, which all Year 7 pupils take during their first term. This introduces different learning styles and strategies and is aimed at:

> ...trying to get the message across from the very beginning that [pupils] *can* learn, they all have the ability to learn, and try[ing] to get them motivated and to understand that, even though they're not all the same in the way that they learn and the speed at which they learn, they all have an ability to make progress and to improve, and it's not a competition – they're improving against their own personal targets.

When questioned about the use of self-assessment in lessons, one pupil pointed out that 'it can detract from how much time you're given in the lesson – if you have to write down [the skills used] then you have less time in the lesson'. On the other hand the pupils appreciated that there was a reason for focusing on these skills. They recognised that 'employers now want everybody to have those basic skills', and explained that:

> we're always encouraged to look ahead and think what we might like to do after leaving school, and then look at what skills we'll need to prepare ourselves for that.

This has a direct benefit in terms of their motivation to learn:

> I find something pointless unless you know there's something you're gonna get out of it.

> It encourages you to look at different subjects in different perspectives.

> It makes you more keen to learn about it... It makes you take it all in.

It is evident that these pupils want to be enthused by their schoolwork. To achieve this end, the second way in which pupils' engagement with their own learning has been brought about is through modification of the ways that subject content is taught. As one teacher explained, the introduction in 2008 of the skills-based curriculum has been instrumental in facilitating this: 'because of the curriculum coming in recently, because it's so open-ended, it allows you to have that slightly more flexibility than before'.

In the science department, the less detailed syllabus for Key Stage 3 has allowed the department to concentrate on creating stronger linkages between Key Stages 2, 3 and 4. There has been an increase in contact with the feeder primaries to allow discussion of the type of work that is set, and a greater range of tasks is now set for pupils at Ysgol David Hughes. In a task on global warming, for example, pupils could be expected to find information from a range of sources and work in groups to create presentations using computer software. The pupils interviewed were extremely enthusiastic about the freedom and variety that this gives them:

> When you're in primary school the teachers design all the experiments, you do them and that's the end of it. But in high school you're given the ... objective but you've got to plan it. You've got a lot more independence.

> ...You've got to figure out how to figure it out...

> In primary you have three hour-sessions just to plan the thing, but here you're quarter of an hour planning it, deciding what you're going to do and then you do it. It's a lot quicker.

> We're given a bit of independence about making our mind up about stuff. The other day in science we were given a load of information, we were told things expand when they're hot and then we had to say why does this happen. ... Our teacher went round every one of us saying if it was right. That was more fun than just being told what was the answer.

Changes in the delivery of mathematics lessons reflect a similar shift towards the delivery of subject-specific content 'little and often'. There is now 'much more emphasis on the skills, so in everything we do how can we bring in the skills, what skills do we want, and what mathematics can we bring into that?' Throughout Years 7 and 8, 'instead of spending three weeks on a certain topic, we're now talking maybe three lessons, [then the] next three lessons, bang, bang, bang, covering skills'.

In addition to bringing in a range of methods in each lesson, as in science, the mathematics department can cover a range of topics in a single lesson. This has been facilitated by the introduction of 'maths mats'. Maths mats are A4 sheets covering real life problems. Each sheet holds a host of information that pupils must draw together to solve the problem. A maths mat, might for example, detail how a farmer is being forced to sell some cows because of the credit crunch; pupils must examine data including each cow's milk yield to determine which cows to sell. Maths mats can also be combined with cookery lessons: a recipe could be written in terms of requiring double the amount of ingredient A as ingredient B.

One of the principal benefits of the mats is that they effectively merge subject and skills content, such that neither is an add-on. The school has worked on mats with the feeder primaries, which has had the dual benefit of improved standardisation of levels and increased continuity of teaching between Years 6 and 7. The benefit of the mats for boys in particular was also highlighted. Boys who 'find some aspects of the work boring in maths really enjoy and are good at this'.

The different approach to a subject needed to engage some boys has also been addressed in the English department. Text choice is seen as particularly important in catching boys' imagination, with texts involving boys as the main characters, especially those who get up to various pranks, and war heroes being especially popular.

Recognising that reading very often falls away once pupils leave primary school, where daily in-class reading is commonplace, the department pushes private reading with all pupils from Year 7. There are reading clubs, book clubs and book auctions, and the librarian has been proactive in introducing new genres and games, so that the 'fun element' is not lost. Pupils also keep reading records, and those who read the required number and range of texts are awarded bronze (Year 7), silver (Year 8) or gold (Year 9) certificates in assembly. For a silver award, a pupil must read ten books, including poetry and a history text.

There are multiple benefits to promoting reading: first and foremost, 'this hopefully establishes an enjoyment of literature as much as anything';

secondly, pupils who read widely see a variety of sentence structures, correct spellings and sophisticated punctuation, 'so it's naturally using their reading to promote their skills and enhance their spelling, punctuation and grammar'; thirdly, it prepares pupils who go on to more advanced study for wider reading and independent study.

Skills days as a response to the skills-based curriculum
One response to the new curriculum detailed by a number of respondents in very positive terms was the introduction of skills days. These days, on which the timetable is suspended to make space for a cross-curricular project that teaches certain skills, are run once per term – in November and February, and for three days at the end of the summer term. On each day, each year group works on a different theme. This initiative has been running for two years, with the initial momentum having been provided by Cynnal. Before the first three-day skills activity, the mathematics department sent a questionnaire to every department. The results were used to identify skills that were receiving less attention in the classroom, and the skills activity was accordingly designed to address these gaps.

The maths, science and geography departments were closely involved in the design of this first activity. The task set, for Year 7 pupils, was to decide which of a series of businesses to locate in which location on the Menai Straight. For the fortnight prior to suspension of the timetable, pupils received lessons preparing them for the task. Then, on day one of the task, they undertook fieldwork. Talks were given by a conservation officer and local business people, and the pupils made geographical sketches, learnt about the history of the crossings and carried out scientific tests on the Straight's waters. On day two, the pupils worked in groups to decide on locations, using SWOT analyses and maths mats. The final day focused on communication and IT skills. During the morning, pupils presented their findings, based on which they were awarded a marketing grant. Depending on the size of grant awarded, they then created a radio or television advertisement for a company.

Teachers reported that pupils' response 'has been incredible', because 'the thing was, the pupils enjoyed it as well – it's not pulling teeth or "you must get these skills into you"'. The pupils themselves were highly enthusiastic about the skills days, mentioning projects including the design and sale of a T-shirt and the pitching of a business idea to 'professional business people'.

As previously discussed, this opportunity to engage with people outside the school on 'real life' projects was particularly valued. Given that the end of the summer term can be 'a time when kids [are] really tired, as well as members of staff', this response is doubly positive.

The decision to go down the road of suspending the timetable for a limited number of days per year is an interesting one. Senior managers at the school are well aware that other schools have changed the Year 7 curriculum more substantially, by joining subjects together to allow thematic teaching in the humanities or arts. Although it was initially thought that this would be a good approach to take at Ysgol David Hughes, having listened to the teaching staff it was decided against:

> You have to go with what suits your establishment... You have to listen to people's opinions because you want people on side and you want them working with you and you want them moving things forward with you. It's a kind of balance.

The school is working to ensure that all subjects contribute to the skills agenda and is finding that, as more departments become involved in the skills days, teachers are increasingly able to see how pupils work in different settings and are feeding that back into the classroom. This approach, characterised by a balance between consistency of approach at the whole-school level and flexibility within the classroom, appears to be very important to the school. The framework that is being developed to support this is discussed in greater detail below. Ultimately, although the curriculum has stayed the same, the implementation of the skills focus has, in the school's view, meant that there has been a shift away from the 'traditional way' of delivering the curriculum.

Addressing underachievement

The skills-based curriculum is proving to be beneficial in tackling underachievement and loss of motivation, as described above. Nevertheless, for the 'minority' of pupils who lose interest in their education during Key Stage 3, a number of additional measures are in place across the school. Indeed, in the current academic year there has been an increased focus on this area, with the school having changed the purpose of its Wednesday after-school club from Year 11 coursework catch-up to underachievement. Pupils can be identified as underachieving by their subject teachers, by heads of year, who look at their progression through the levels, or by other members of the senior management team, who track both department-wide trends and individual pupil performance.

Teachers described their monitoring systems in terms of a matrix in which pupils' performance in the range of required skills is mapped by level. In this way not only can teachers be sure that all skills are covered by each pupil, but it also enables them to spot areas where further development is needed. Thus a pupil with Level 6 in all skill areas except one, in which he or she has a Level 5, will receive targeted support to improve that area.

Further to these teacher-specific and department-wide systems, the headteacher has been working on a new school-wide framework for monitoring. A data sheet is now kept for every pupil in Years 7-11. Subject teachers are responsible for passing on individual targets to pupils, which they record in their own diaries. This can be compared with actual achievement after each assessment period. Newly introduced in the current academic year, in addition to these targets, each pupil is given 'two positives' per subject: these are detailed areas for improvement, such as focusing on paragraphing in English, that will help them to achieve their target.

At the end of each assessment period effort and achievement grades are recorded for every pupil. The totals of pupils achieving Level 5 are calculated. These data are shared with heads of department, heads of year and tutors. Heads of year will discuss the data with form tutors, who then discuss targets and achievement with individual pupils during dedicated registration periods once every half term. These extended registration periods last for 25 minutes each over the course of one week. They are a new initiative implemented following recognition that:

> the tutor is in a unique position, because they've actually got access to the data across all the subjects, and they've also got the child sitting there with a diary so they can then actually look at where it is that common patterns are arising, and maybe pinpoint that.

Meanwhile, heads of department receive the overview for their subject, allowing them to compare actual performance against targets, and are also able to compare pupils' performance in their own subject against all other KS3 subjects. Where pupils are seen to be underachieving in that subject, discussions will be held both with the subject teacher and on a departmental basis to identify suitable strategies and solutions.

A variety of additional strategies is used to address underachievement, depending on who the identified pupil is, the age of the pupil and what subject he or she is underachieving in. If multiple pupils are identified in one subject, the school can set up an after-school study group to set them back on track. For individuals facing difficulties, the school might invite his or her parents to discuss the situation. It also has the ability to assign a learning coach. Whilst the work of the learning coaches, who currently number three, has been undertaken for a number of years, their title and role were reviewed during the past academic year. Learning coaches work with pupils who are underachieving for non-additional learning needs related issues including long-term absence, family issues or social problems. The majority of support is provided on a one-to-one basis, with some additional in-class support. One learning coach is assigned to each of Key Stages 3, 4 and 5.

Transition into a bilingual school
In response to Estyn's finding that 'the primary sector haven't had the support in assessing or giving the levels to the pupils [that] the secondary teachers have had over the last few years', much of the school's transition work is currently concentrated on the standardisation of attainment levels with the feeder primaries.

This process was described as 'a bit further down the line' in mathematics than in other subjects. The introduction of maths mats provided the department with an opportunity to work in partnership with the primaries, with each school creating a maths mat which was then levelled by the other schools. This led to standardisation of marks for each mat and, through that, to a shared understanding of the required skills and associated levels. In science this process has been led by the Cynnal science advisor, who has been working with every catchment area in Anglesey and Gwynedd during the past academic year. As previously mentioned, the English department have also been working with Cynnal, on a more informal basis. In Welsh, the school is part of the WJEC's moderation pilot project. The school has come together in a group with others to assess individual pupils' portfolios, in a bid to 'tighten the interpretation of a level'. A portfolio of work has now been sent to the WJEC for accreditation.

The increase in contact with the feeder primaries was described as 'of great use' for two reasons. Firstly, it has provided Ysgol David Hughes with more detailed information about the standard attained by pupils in Year 6. One teacher explained that 'it was nice to actually receive examples of work from the primary ... just so that we have an idea of what depth of understanding they have and then to what level we can then progress those children'. For this reason, an understanding of the pupils that extends beyond the single figure of attainment level was valued by all the teachers to whom we spoke.

There is an additional value to obtaining this information for the Welsh department, since the school groups pupils on entry according to their standard of Welsh. As a bilingual school, Ysgol David Hughes must give primacy to the linguistic skills of its pupils so as to ensure that they are able to follow the curriculum whilst also being challenged to progress in both languages. The aim is 'to make sure that they end their school era with an equal competency in English and Welsh', and over 70% of pupils now sit Welsh as a first language exam in Year 11.

The school has an eight form entry. Three forms, predominantly containing pupils from a Welsh-speaking background but with some other pupils with a high level of second-language competency, are taught on a 70:30 split between Welsh and English. A further three forms are taught 50:50; most of these pupils are highly competent in Welsh, but tend to revert to English if not challenged by their teachers. The final two forms are taught 70% of their time in English and the remainder in Welsh. This represents a more formal approach to bilingualism than was originally the case. Whereas teachers were once able to choose a language based on 'beliefs and personality and teachers' strengths', there is now a consistent policy that requires departments to specify in which language each module will be taught.

Described as 'complex' and 'really difficult', it is clear that incorporating bilingualism introduces a significant additional challenge for teaching staff and management. The basic eight form language-based division, for example, is complicated by the fact that attention is also given to non-linguistic ability in the core subjects of English, maths and science. Some pupils might find themselves in a predominantly English medium class having only recently moved to Wales. Others will be in this class because of their lower ability and consequent inability to work in two languages. To ensure that very able pupils with Welsh as a second language are sufficiently challenged, the school has implemented some ability banding. Beyond this, however, the emphasis is on differentiation within lessons according to individual pupils' abilities.

The second benefit of increased contact with the feeder schools has been greater continuity of teaching styles and lesson content between Years 6 and 7. A bridging unit is undertaken in English, focusing on newspaper and magazine styles and, in Year 7, incorporating celebrity-style interviewing between pupils to maintain motivation; pupils are taught about layout, writing in a lively and entertaining style and engaging the audience. In maths, pupils are introduced to maths mats at primary school. In science, discussions about the type of work undertaken in each school have informed the way in which Year 7 and 8 units are taught, and discussions are currently underway with the Cynnal science advisor about creating a bridging unit in science that would be 'quite hands on'.

Pupils are also introduced to new subjects. Members of the German department teach a series of six lessons in the primaries during the summer term, and a similar course has previously been run in French. Much of this activity has a pastoral as well as a pedagogic role in the transition process. Sessions for Year 6 pupils in P.E., computing, woodwork and drama allow pupils to get to know teachers and the school environment, and also enthuse them about the transition. As one pupil said of her experience taking drama, 'I thought it was different. I like acting, and I thought "oh, so there's interesting stuff in this school too", because there wasn't drama in primary school'. Between visits by teachers to the primaries and by pupils to Ysgol David Hughes, there is therefore 'quite a bit of contact' prior to the start of Year 7. Drawing together smooth pastoral transition and continuity of teaching with pupil engagement, the school also sends its sixth form students to run projects in the primary schools as part of their Welsh baccalaureate. This has apparently been a source of educational benefit and enjoyment for both sets of pupils and has improved the confidence of Year 7 pupils.

Literacy support
The special educational needs coordinator (SENCO) also visits the primary schools to become acquainted with Year 5 and 6 pupils with additional learning needs. The SENCO will get to know all pupils with a statement or who are registered under Anglesey's three star system, which is a step down from statementing. She will then liaise with the head of year over class allocations. Pupils with additional needs are grouped into smaller classes of ideally 12-15, and no more than eighteen, children.

The school has fifteen learning support assistants who assist with classes in all years. Usually no more than four assistants per year will follow a statemented pupil from primary school. The remainder can be allocated as the school sees fit, and the policy is to target support, which works out at two assistants per year group. 'Rarely' do these LSAs double up with the one-to-one support assistants in a class. Because the school aims to encourage independence, depending on the specific needs of the pupil requiring one-to-one support the LSA might also move around the classroom to help other pupils.

One of the school's support assistants has also begun to take the stronger pupils from the lower set Welsh group out of class in Years 9 and 10. She uses this opportunity to push this group to higher attainment, using work provided by the class teacher. It was suggested that she might in future begin to take a small group of Year 7 pupils from lessons in order to work on basic skills. The change to the curriculum that has allowed secondary school pupils to be taught material from KS2 or, if necessary, KS1, was highlighted as being extremely beneficial, as teachers will be able to start from the beginning again and build the foundations for progression onto KS3 material. This is now being put into practice both in small groups and on a one-to-one basis.

In order to target literacy support, all Year 7s are tested on reading and spelling in both languages. Those with a reading age below nine attend reading club, which is run four mornings per week in the library by sixth form reading buddies. The spelling club, which has a similar cut-off age, uses computer software. Where possible this runs throughout Years 7-9, although 'we tend to find that our numbers are too high and we can't cope maybe with pupils from Year 9 as well, so it tends to be Years 7 and 8'. From an intake of approximately 180, 60 pupils are receiving support in the current academic year. Although 'it would've been nice to include more', limited resources make this impossible. It is interesting to note that two thirds of those given support require help in English, and the remainder Welsh. This was variously attributed to the 'phonetic aspect of Welsh which makes it easier' and to the fact that pupils 'get so much Welsh in the primary schools ... I think it's very often English where they do need that extra push'.

For those pupils who do not sufficiently increase their reading age in reading club, the school has introduced the Catch Up programme, which is run by the SENCO and an LSA. In the last academic year nine Year 7 pupils used the programme. It has proved so successful that only one has stayed on into

Year 8. Catch Up requires two fifteen minute sessions per week, for which pupils are withdrawn from class, with every effort made to avoid withdrawal from the core subjects. An equal emphasis is placed on reading, spelling and oracy, although the specific tasks to be completed can be tailored according to a pupil's individual needs. The fifteen minute lessons – which are strictly controlled using a timer – were described as highly effective:

> I think it's better really, myself, because I think you've got their concentration, they know it's fifteen minutes... They can see the time counting down and they know "right, I've only got six minutes of this". They're on board, they're on target, they know what they're doing. I think that's quite enough, because I think you'd lose their concentration otherwise. Fifteen minutes is just a nice time – you don't lose them at the end of it.

This view was echoed by the respondent's colleague, who feels at the moment that short bursts of intensive teaching work best, and that having four fifteen minute lessons per week helps the new information to 'stick'.

Further to these targeted interventions, the school is increasingly ensuring that literacy is a focus across all subjects. As well as the extended writing task for all subjects that is being planned in conjunction with Cynnal, as discussed above, there is now a whole-school marking policy. This ensures that pupils are required to meet high standards of literacy in all subjects and that they receive consistent messages. Concerns about the grammatical skills of the current Year 7 have also prompted preliminary discussions on how best they might be improved.

Future priorities
Together with the more developed initiatives detailed here, this can be seen as evidence of the school's commitment, described at the top of this chapter, to further improvement. One respondent expressed the current situation thus:

> There's quite a few 'watch this spaces' around the school. There's been a shift in the personnel in school as well, so a change in personnel sometimes comes with new ideas I suppose. And there's obviously new initiatives that we need to take note of as

well. Very much work in progress, I think.

For example, a series of after-school clubs – which will involve pupils requiring help with literacy and homework as well as those with interests in crafts, robotics and foreign languages, and will therefore hopefully reduce the stigma surrounding extra support – are being introduced. However, whilst one senior manager acknowledged that:

> it's really important that we don't just accept [that] we've got a certain plateau now. We want to improve and we want the pupils to get better and better results.

she also described the school's approach going forward in terms of:

> ...not doing anything radically different to what we were doing before. ... We're just tightening up or sharpening up on certain aspects.

The recent introduction of school-wide monitoring is the principal manifestation of this 'sharpening up'. The school recognises that 'we all develop at different times and what works for one might not work for another', and anticipates that the monitoring system will enable teachers and senior management to 'get to the individual pupil' in a way that will maximise his or her potential.

Chapter 10:
Ysgol y Preseli

School performance at KS3

Described in its 2008 inspection report as 'a very good school with many outstanding features'[30], Ysgol y Preseli scored the highest grade in each of the seven key inspection questions. This performance clearly feeds into the school's assessment results. Contextual value added data analysis showed that Ysgol y Preseli added statistically significant value from Key Stage 2 to Key Stage 3 in two of the three years 2006-2008.

The latest figures available for the school show that the proportion of pupils achieving English Level 5 or above at Key Stage 3 in 2010 was, at 94%, twenty-three percentage points above the 2009 national average[31]. The corresponding figure for Welsh was 84%, nine points above the all-Wales average, for mathematics was 98%, twenty-four points above, and for science was 91%, fifteen points above the average. At 89%, the proportion of pupils achieving the core subject indicator was 25 points above the 2010 Wales average[32].

At Key Stage 4, results remain well above the national and local authority averages. Eighty-two percent of pupils achieved the Level 2 threshold in 2010, compared with 62% across the whole of Pembrokeshire and 64% in Wales as a whole. Although this falls to 64% when A*-C passes in English or Welsh and mathematics are included, a similar drop nationwide means that the school still outperforms the national average by 15 percentage points[31].

---

30   Estyn, 2008, Inspection under Section 28 of the Education Act 2005, A Report on the Quality of Education in Ysgol Gyfun Ddwyieithog Y Preseli.

31   Ysgol y Preseli, 2010, Governors' Annual Report.

32   www.statswales.wales.gov.uk, Schools and Teachers, Examinations and Statistics, School-level Reports, Secondary School Level Data.

Creating a positive ethos

Central to the school's success according to its own analysis is the ethos which staff and pupils work together to achieve. Ysgol y Preseli's stated aims emphasise the importance of tolerance and respect for oneself, for others and for moral and religious values. They further describe the school's role as being 'to develop a good character in the pupils and to teach them to live a good life after school', and to nurture 'virtues' including courtesy, honesty, perseverance and conscientiousness[33]. In citing these goals, the school makes clear that achievement of academic potential forms just one part of pupils' development as rounded individuals.

On visiting Ysgol y Preseli, it was evident that this ethos pervades the daily life of the school. Respect – for others, for the school building and for resources – was described by one member of the senior management team as being 'very high profile'. It is achieved through a combination of strict enforcement and positive reinforcement. For example, there are:

> ... standards [in how] we expect [pupils] to speak to staff. They are punished if they do speak [out of turn] to staff. And they know that.

However, whilst sanctions are implemented where necessary, greater emphasis is placed on the carrot rather than the stick. This same staff member acknowledged that it is not possible to create a positive ethos overnight and described how activities such as the annual Eisteddfod and daily morning assemblies serve both to reinforce expectations of pupils and to create a positive atmosphere. Notions of 'pride' and 'respect' were not only repeatedly referred to by teaching staff, but also informed pupils' comments. As one pupil explained:

> [Ysgol y Preseli] is like a family. I know it's a cliche, but ... the whole school is just as one.

The Welsh medium aspect of the school was deemed to have an important impact, bringing the school and community together through a shared sense of 'Welshness'. The fact that some children travel thirty miles each way to attend Preseli was seen as evidence of the commitment of families

---

33   Ysgol y Preseli, 2010, Prospectus 2010-2011.

to the school and its Welsh language provision. More generally, the school was described as the 'focal point' of the local community, with the support given by 'a very, very high percentage' of parents and members of the local community being described as 'fantastic'. One example of this support that was offered was the raising of over £8000 at the school's Christmas fair.

Parental involvement in pupils' *academic* progression is also a 'key issue' at Ysgol y Preseli. The school believes, for instance, that it is essential for parents to 'buy into' ongoing learning in the home:

> We do ask [pupils] to read at home. You need ten minutes reading in English or in Welsh at home, and sometimes you need a parent to sit with them to listen.

'Changes in homes and families' have meant that this appears to be happening less often than has previously been the case. Moreover, where parents are having problems with children at home they often expect the school to address those problems, in spite of the relatively short amount of time that pupils spend in the classroom. It is therefore becoming increasingly important for the school to find effective ways of working *with* parents and of addressing welfare and wellbeing concerns. Ysgol y Preseli has identified this as an important focus for the near future, as discussed in greater detail below.

Although a high level of parental support cannot be presumed upon going forward, the school hopes to maintain a good relationship with parents. Nevertheless, staff also place a great deal of store by good pupil-teacher relations, through which they aim to foster a positive learning environment within the school. Pupils and staff each have clearly defined roles which contribute to this relationship.

Pupil engagement with the life of the school is characterised by a high level of trust and expectation, with one of the most telling roles in this regard being the contribution of the School Council to staff appointments. Sixth form members of the Council described how they interview candidates individually, before feeding back their opinions to the Board of Governors. Whilst the questions asked of candidates vary according to the post, past interviews have focused on what candidates feel they could bring to the school and how they would make the subject more fun for pupils, with candidates for senior management posts also asked to explain what new policies they would seek to implement.

Older pupils also play an important part in the pastoral support system for younger pupils. Each new pupil is paired up with a sixth form 'buddy', to whom they can take any questions or problems. According to one current buddy:

> most of the time [younger pupils] are pretty happy to talk to teachers, but we are there for support because we've all been through it, so they know they're talking to someone they can relate to.

In addition to the formal buddy system, older pupils showed themselves to be aware of a more general responsibility for others. Sixth formers monitor the lunch queues, which provides 'a really good chance' for younger pupils to talk to the older ones. It is also an opportunity for older pupils to spot potential problems. One sixth former reflected that:

> I know now if I see someone looking sad or looking alone, you can see that this person might need someone to talk to. I think now it's a responsibility of mine as a sixth former to go and see if this person's alright. I think that's something that is taught throughout the school, so that's really good.

This degree of care for others is a particularly striking aspect of the atmosphere within the school, and suggests that the stated ethos is being played out in practice. Further evidence of the school ethos being put into practice is provided by teachers' discussion of their commitment to seeing pupils develop. As a head of department explained:

> the majority of us don't mind opening our departments over the Easter holidays or teaching here until half past six for different clubs, because we enjoy it. We enjoy being in the company of our pupils.

The extra demands that this attitude places on teachers was highlighted by her colleague, who nevertheless acknowledged the necessity of such commitment:

> Teachers are prepared to go the extra mile. ... You have to do it: the after-school revision classes, clubs, the giving up of days of

the Easter holidays etcetera. Yes it is tough. We do expect a lot of the staff. But the reward is the success that you get ultimately at the end of the journey. So there's a professional fulfilment for staff. ... You could go into the staffroom and they would say this is a school where the demands on the teaching staff are quite high. But if you're going to sustain standards ... you have to buy into that culture. There's that element of teamwork that makes sure that we continue to thrive.

This reference to teamwork would seem to be particularly important, because it is only through widespread buy-in to this culture that consistency of approach can be achieved.

Pupils confirmed that 'one of the best things' about Preseli is the 'fantastic' relationship between pupils and teachers. They reported that 'teachers are willing to put in the extra time' to assist pupils who require additional help with their studies, and also noted that teachers' interest in their pupils extends beyond the classroom: 'Teachers take an interest in what the students do outside of school, and give them praise. ... Teachers bother to stop in the corridor and ask how it's going.' This was seen to have a motivational effect: 'It makes the whole environment a better place to be in. You want to please them, to work to do well in school.'

Targets and rewards
Many of the extra-curricular activities in which pupils take part are run by the school itself. These include lunchtime clubs such as Clwb Hwyl, 5x60 sports club, English reading and writing clubs, and sewing and 'Glee' clubs. One pupil who had moved to the school in the previous year felt, despite having come from 'quite a similar' school, that Ysgol y Preseli provides more opportunities to get involved in the life of the school. She had already taken part in public speaking and the putting on of shows.

According to a member of the senior management team, large numbers of pupils make use of the various extra-curricular opportunities. Extra-curricular activities are open to all pupils, but staff make a particular effort to encourage 'high fliers' to become involved. This adds a further dimension to the most talented pupils' education, and supplements actions that are encouraged within the more formal learning environment – such as reading around the set texts.

Recognition of achievement in these activities, and in activities undertaken in the community, is not limited to informal acknowledgement by teaching staff. The school also makes a point of giving formal praise in assemblies and at the annual prize evening. Referring to having received a prize in assembly, one pupil said:

> It's happened once or twice ... it's a really nice feeling to have people clapping. I think even sat in the audience you think to yourself it'd be nice to go up on stage. It does entice some sort of wanting to improve yourself.

Pupils regarded the prize evening as another 'good way of rewarding pupils'. Prizes are awarded not only for achievement, but also for effort, attendance and improvement, allowing all pupils to aspire to receiving an award.

Pupils' progress is assessed against targets that are set both by subject teachers and by the pupils themselves. Each term, pupils set themselves two or three targets, which can be general – for instance to read more – or more specific – relating to areas for improvement in a particular subject. Progress towards these targets is assessed through self-evaluation at the end of the term, with any unmet targets being set again for the following term. These are supplemented by grade-based targets and expectations set by teachers. The importance of making sure that pupils understand the reasons for the targets that have been set was emphasised by one teacher, as was the need for at least one positive achievement to be noted for each piece of work.

Each of these ends requires teachers to take account of individual pupils' strengths and weaknesses in their subject area. In addition to frequent assessment, which is discussed below, this is facilitated by regular one-to-one meetings with pupils at which teacher targets are discussed and pupils are assisted in setting their own goals. The balance between pupils' responsibility for their own progression and teacher input was one acknowledged by the pupils themselves. One quoted the school motto – "cofia ddysgu byw", or "remember to learn how to live" – and explained how it emphasised the importance of becoming a rounded individual and, ultimately, of gaining independence, whilst another added that 'it's important to say that, although independence is encouraged, guidance is always there to help you make those decisions'.

These meetings take place with subject teachers, but all pupils at Key Stages 4 and 5 are also assigned an individual learning mentor. This is a teacher who looks at a pupil's overall performance and meets with him or her each half term to discuss progress. One benefit of the learning mentor system is the mentor's ability to take an overview of all subjects and pinpoint particular strengths and weaknesses. Pupils further mentioned that they value the opportunity to discuss practical methods for reaching their individual targets.

Building on the success of this approach at KS4 and KS5, the school is in the process of working out the logistics so as to be able to introduce learning mentors for Key Stage 3 pupils in September 2011. According to a member of the senior management team, introduction of mentors for KS3 pupils also ties into the learner wellbeing agenda, which has been highlighted as being of particular importance going forward. The school is 'picking up more and more issues regarding [pupils'] emotional wellbeing', and believes that helping pupils to develop their emotional intelligence will be 'a key aspect of them developing as effective learners'. Learning mentors will play an important part in this, although discussions are underway about whether additional pastoral teams, focusing specifically on emotional wellbeing, should be developed in addition.

Learning and assessment
The setting of targets by pupils is part of an explicit policy of developing Assessment for Learning techniques within Ysgol y Preseli. A variety of strategies, including self-assessment, peer assessment in pairs or small groups and whole-class assessment led by the class teacher, is employed. Pupils are also asked to assess their own progress at the end of each unit, and to provide feedback on the unit itself for the benefit of future classes.

In Year 9, a particular focus on the key skill of Improving Own Learning and Performance is introduced. One respondent described how this focus is proving to be beneficial in practical subjects such as art:

> We encourage pupils to be aware that ... if they haven't got natural ability that doesn't matter. [What matters is] that they can see that they've progressed and that there is an improvement in their skills. [That may be] not just their practical or their creative skills, but that they can discuss the work of an artist, or they can

discuss their own work with other pupils, or that they have ... an understanding of art within the culture that they live in. ... They're aware that, with regard to their own learning and improvement, they can improve on their different skills. They're allowed to have an aim and objective, and it's all very personal to them.

Pupils' own knowledge of skills and recognition of how and when they have been applied is an area to which special attention is being paid. This is an ongoing challenge: pupils are now 'very fluent in the vocabulary linked to the skills', but 'one of the things that learners find the most difficult is if you ask how?'. There is therefore 'work to do' on 'enabling pupils to recognise what strategies they have used to improve their learning'.

To this end, the school is currently developing its own Habits of Mind agenda. The Habits of Mind approach encourages the development of the skills and strategies that most effectively enable people to meet challenges. Thus children will be encouraged to reflect on how they have achieved success in a given task. Was it, for example, because they were persistent? Did they manage impulsiveness? Were they focused and did they stop to think about what they needed to do? Having identified what led to a particular success, pupils will be encouraged to transfer this approach to other situations. This agenda is being taken forward by the school's own professional learning community but, since it is also part of a county-wide focus, the school will be able to work in tandem with the local authority and other schools which adopt the approach.

The school regards itself as 'traditional' in that, in addition to regular end-of-unit tests, it holds formal examinations twice per year. One member of the senior management team explained that, although there was no imperative to have 'sit-down' exams, they are used because they focus pupils and provide a 'snapshot' of where they are at present and how they are progressing. When asked to explain what factors make Ysgol y Preseli a good school, one pupil immediately responded by praising the value of frequent testing:

It really helps you to understand the level you're at, and it really does keep you going because it's less of a shock when the exam comes. You feel more prepared for the exam and you feel like you know what you're doing and you can just get on with it.

The outcomes of these formal tests inform the self-assessment and target-setting processes, so feeding in to efforts to ensure a constant upward trajectory for all pupils throughout their time at Preseli.

Curricular innovations

Ysgol y Preseli is a predominantly Welsh-medium school. Pupils have the option of taking mathematics and science lessons through the medium of English, with all other subjects taught in Welsh. Approximately two thirds of pupils take science in English. In mathematics, which uses a lower level of subject-specific language, an increasing number of pupils are learning in Welsh. At present, the division is approximately fifty-fifty. The school is particularly proud of its pupils' bilingualism, the school's contribution to which was recognised in the last Estyn inspection.

Year 7 pupils are set for Welsh, English and mathematics. Science classes are not set at Key Stage 3. In Welsh this is a new departure, resulting from an influx of significantly lower ability pupils in the current year group. The usual practice is for mixed ability teaching of Welsh in Year 7, with the exception of a single higher ability group containing pupils with good first language Welsh, followed by setting in Year 8. Maths sets are decided based on Year 6 results, whilst the English department takes September to assess pupil abilities before introducing sets. In all cases pupils study the same themes and undertake the same tasks, but at a different pace.

Senior management at Ysgol y Preseli claim that they are 'not offering a radical approach to Key Stage 3', in the sense that they are not planning to develop an integrated curriculum through the merging of subjects. The possibility of merging subjects has been discussed, but 'at the moment we feel that the learning climate that we've created here is a successful one, so we're not going to change that'.

Two reasons for this decision were put forward. Firstly, the school does not want to risk damaging the strong learning ethos that it has built up; qualitative and quantitative data show that 'what we're doing currently is working', and there is a reluctance to make alterations that might jeopardise this. Secondly, management are focused on ensuring that a balance remains between teaching of skills and of subject-specific knowledge. This is deemed necessary as pupils move towards Key Stage 4, since many GCSE courses are highly 'knowledge-based'. Whilst staff admit that a 'radical' approach to the KS3 curriculum might serve to improve some pupils' uptake of skills, 'there's a degree of risk' to wholesale change that is neither desirable nor necessary:

> The innovation here is strong enough within the departments [and] the existing curriculum. I think that's convinced us not to go for a more radical curriculum at Key Stage 3.

There has, nevertheless, been ongoing change within lessons in response to the skills-based curriculum. Year 7 pupils reported that they had been exposed to a range of different teaching methods since arriving at Preseli. Lessons might, for example, contain a mix of individual and partner-based activities, or small group working. Computers are often used in lessons, allowing pupils to undertake independent research, and pupils recognised that they were fortunate in having access to laptops which can be used in any class. They also appreciated less formal activities such as the playing of games in maths lessons.

Older pupils were particularly keen on opportunities for 'open discussion' in lessons. Brainstorming questions in the lead up to exams, discussion of the context for what is being taught and advice on wider reading were all mentioned. The importance of providing a context for what is taught can seemingly not be overestimated. One pupil explained that 'if I don't understand something, I don't want to know, so by giving us better understanding it makes us want to learn more', whilst another – referring to having the future applicability of knowledge explained to him – said that this 'inspires you to do better. ... If someone tells you why you need it, when you need it, it inspires you to try harder and do well'. Common to all the learning methods discussed by the pupils is that each introduces an element of 'fun' to learning. As one sixth former stated:

> if you make lessons more fun, you're still learning but you don't notice that you're learning. ... You're learning through having fun, which I think is a really vital part of school. It's not just learning by the book, just opening a text book. ... I think it's important that we have different ways of learning.

Addressing underachievement
The proportion of pupils not engaged in learning through these methods is

described by senior management as small. According to one member of the senior management team, 'we're very, very fortunate here. You're talking, within a year group of 160 for example, about four or five students, mostly boys, mostly at Key Stage 4.' Regular monitoring of all pupils' progress is an important means of rapidly identifying those pupils who need additional support through the mentoring system. The assignment of targets for, and by, individual pupils is also beneficial; because pupils know what their targets are, 'they know what they're working towards', making them less likely to 'get lost in all these GCSEs'.

As well as its learning mentors, Ysgol y Preseli has further dedicated staff who can assist with addressing the root causes of underachievement. A designated youth worker works closely with the school, and there is also a behavioural support teacher. Both of these work together to provide opportunities for pupils in lunchtime clubs and through mini-projects. The school is also engaged, in partnership with the Urdd, in the Reach the Heights programme – an initiative designed to address disengagement – through which pupils can gain OCN Level 1 accreditation. Some pupils are also released from lessons at Preseli one day per week, during which time they follow more vocational subjects, such as construction, engineering or car mechanics, at the local college. The school is also working closely with the Engage 14-19 team who assist the school in providing opportunities for those students in danger of becoming disaffected.

One respondent admitted that engaging with the hardest to reach pupils can be challenging, but stressed that the school's aim is to work *with* them. At the same time, high expectations are set for all pupils – the number of entry level courses at Key Stage 4 is being cut back – and teachers 'are always pleasantly surprised' at how well they achieve. Thus, although some pupils might be slightly disengaged from the curriculum, the school is 'helping them to make sure that they have got skills and formal qualifications'. Feedback from colleges is invariably positive, 'because they are quite well-rounded individuals'. It was evident that this is something that individual teachers and the school as a whole take pride in.

Literacy and basic skills

In ensuring that all pupils reach a good level of basic skills before leaving, the school addresses significant resources towards two groups. In addition, all pupils work towards key skills accreditation, as described below. The first of the two groups receiving additional support comprises pupils with a reading age below nine years on entry; these pupils require intensive support and often have other educational needs. The second group, known as the 'target group', consists of pupils with reading ages between nine and eleven years. From a cohort of approximately 160 pupils in the current Year 7, thirty-one have been found to have a reading age below their chronological age in Welsh and thirty-seven in English, with thirteen pupils operating below their chronological age in numeracy.

Pupils in the first group, with the most serious basic skills deficits, are withdrawn from two lessons per week. Ysgol y Preseli has lessons of 35 or 40 minutes in duration and so, by the time pupils are settled in their basic skills class, this allows for an intensive 25 minutes of focused support in literacy – in Welsh and English – and numeracy. Pair work has been found to be preferable to one-to-one support in many cases, because it gives pupils confidence. A number of pupils in the current Year 7 have significant problems with the alphabet and are unable to spell the days of the week in Welsh. Given these extremely poor linguistic skills, the school has deemed it a priority to focus on improving ability in this group.

The high number of pupils with a serious literacy deficit in the current Year 7 has meant that it has not been possible to withdraw the 'target group' from lessons during the first term. Pupils in this group receive in-class support from a learning support assistant. Although these pupils do not have such serious needs, withdrawal can nevertheless be extremely beneficial. In order to be able to withdraw them from lessons in the second term for pair work, the school envisaged reducing withdrawal for the first group to once per week.

This arrangement for support has come about because of a particularly weak cohort. According to the deputy headteacher, who has responsibility for literacy, the variability across years requires the school to take a flexible approach to support, one that 'moves and changes according to the results of retesting and also according to the numbers that we have every year'. In every year, the intention is to ensure that only 'dwindling numbers' of pupils require support in Year 8.

The school has recently lost three of its learning support assistants who, due to resource constraints, will not be replaced. There is currently an LSA in each of Years 7, 8, 9 and 10, with two assigned to Year 11 pupils and one in the sixth form. With the exception of the assistant in Year 7, each of the LSAs is assigned to a specific pupil. Other pupils in these classes also benefit, however: in Year 8, for example, the LSA is attached to one pupil but also works closely with two others, particularly when the class is involved in small group work. The Year 7 assistant works with the whole of the special needs class, which usually numbers around ten or twelve pupils. There are currently no plans to further reduce the number of LSAs but, were further cutbacks to occur, since there is only a statutory requirement to provide LSAs for statemented pupils the support for this class would be most likely to be lost.

Ysgol y Preseli is unusual in the Pembrokeshire area for also having subject-specific LSAs. Until recently, the school had LSAs with special expertise in Welsh, English, mathematics and special needs. Following the departure of the Welsh LSA, the assistant with special needs expertise combines this role with that of Welsh LSA. Both the English and the Welsh LSAs now work with the 'target group' and the special needs class, whereas previously they were only working with the 'target group'. The English assistant also takes pupils out of registration periods on days when there is no assembly. The workload has increased significantly for the remaining LSAs. Referring to the work of the English LSA, the deputy headteacher said: 'I don't know how many children she sees ... they're flat out'.

Described as 'key to everything' is that the support assistants 'want to see the child developing'. In addition to the good relationship between LSAs and pupils, the school has been working to ensure that pupils who are withdrawn from lessons receive positive reinforcement from their teachers:

> Sometimes there is a stigma when you take a child out of a lesson. I've been trying to tell staff not to let it be negative. Don't say 'why are you leaving again?'. Say 'what are you reading now?'. Be positive. It's like leaving for a violin lesson – the intervention programme ... is the same as that. I think the general attitude of staff towards literacy and numeracy intervention programmes has changed, it's more positive.

At the whole-school level, all pupils are now able to gain key skills accreditation. This process began with accreditation at Key Stage 5 over ten years ago, before being rolled out across the school. According to the deputy headteacher, far more important than the accreditation itself is that pupils are aware of the six key skills and are able to implement them in their learning. Looking to the future, Ysgol y Preseli believes that the key skills focus will facilitate transition for pupils who have experienced the Foundation Phase. This focus was characterised by one assistant headteacher as part of an emphasis on innovation, imagination and creativity, combined with making sure that pupils have 'the basics'.

A further part of the whole-school approach to skills is the use of sixth formers as literacy and numeracy 'buddies'. On mornings when there is no assembly, whole year groups will spend ten to fifteen minutes working on their literacy or numeracy. One term is spent on reading in English, one term on reading in Welsh and one term on numeracy-based puzzles. Sixth formers move around their assigned classroom, along with the LSAs and class tutor, listening to and working with the pupils.

Achieving consistency of practice

With respect to teaching and learning strategies, senior management at Ysgol y Preseli acknowledge that there is 'a tremendous amount of good practice' in the school. They also recognise, however, that there is variation across the school and that this needs to be reduced in order to improve standards. To this end, an extensive programme of lesson observation is taking place. This initiative is being coordinated by a recently convened professional learning community (PLC) for teaching and learning. It allows both for teachers to observe each other within and across departments, and for senior management to monitor practice.

Opportunities for staff to observe colleagues' lessons are made possible by the use of local authority funds and of Welsh Government Better Schools Fund monies to release teachers from other commitments for the duration. The school has moved away from a situation where only heads of department conduct observations, and all staff are encouraged to observe each other. One head of department reported that she was now more aware of the strengths and weaknesses of staff in her department, meaning that she could arrange for them to observe relevant lessons and staff members anywhere in the school. This is helping to move the school from a situation in which pockets of good practice exist to one of 'more consistency across the board'.

Members of the senior management team continue to conduct lesson observation, for the dual purpose of improving standards within departments and increasing consistency at the whole-school level. Observation is conducted by department and occurs on a three-year cycle. Over the period of a fortnight, a sample of lessons from all teachers and across the year groups is observed. The number of lessons observed depends on the size of the department and is also limited by the time available to senior managers; recent monitoring of the science department included a total sample of twenty-one lessons, with each teacher being observed on approximately two occasions. Teachers' files, resources and assessment records are also examined.

Feedback is then given to the teachers. According to an assistant headteacher:

> the feedback session is as important as the actual observation process itself. It's almost a coaching culture, really. We're touching on something that's very, very important – the culture of openness. Traditionally ... anybody who comes in is a threat to [teachers'] autonomy within their environment. ... What we're trying to create is that culture of openness and honesty. It's very difficult to accept feedback in a non-critical way, but that's what we're aiming for.

To achieve this, the feedback session is designed to lead towards a consensus between the teacher, his or her head of department and the observer. The final grading of the lessons is the result of an agreement reached between all three parties. When this process was first introduced, staff displayed some degree of scepticism, because the observing managers were not necessarily subject specialists. However, the focus in feedback sessions on the process rather than the subject content of lessons, and on the strengths of the lessons and how to build on them, has helped to make the process – in one teacher's words – 'very, very positive'.

At the departmental level, lesson observation feeds into the creation of an action plan. This provides a timetable for agreed improvements to teaching and learning practice. The action plan is based on a report containing the conclusions of the observation period. As in the feedback sessions, this report and the action plan must both be the result of agreement between the department and senior management team. Heads of department are given the opportunity to add to or remove from the report, and the teaching staff are thus able to retain control over the process. Throughout the process, the emphasis on 'openness in that discussion and dialogue', means that 'we can move forward together'.

One of the most innovative aspects of the school's efforts to improve consistency of practice is the decision to begin videoing good practice in the classroom. The PLC members have decided to film because 'it's quite difficult to put down [what makes an effective lesson] on paper':

> It's quite easy to say that for an exceptional lesson we want to see this, this, this and this. But when you see it in practice, you get a better idea of what makes an exceptional lesson.

Examples of good practice in starting and developing lessons, of excellent plenaries, and of engaging pupils and giving them responsibility for their own learning will be recorded. Members of the PLC also plan to create and record a 'traditional' lesson based on the 'chalk and talk' approach. Together these will be the starting point for discussions among staff about the most valid forms of lesson structure and delivery.

Effective use of resources
The creation of a professional learning community for teaching and learning at Ysgol y Preseli has served to focus attention on sharing good practice internally, but this has not stopped the school from looking elsewhere for sector-leading practice as well. This includes its engagement with practice in the data family of schools and work with the local authority-level Effective Learning Group – which consists of staff from the primary and secondary sectors – on shared agendas such as Assessment for Learning and Habits of Mind. In addition to allowing the school to tap into external expertise, this strategy plays an important role in the effective use of increasingly limited resources. Thus, for example, rather than multiple schools in the county sending individuals to conferences, they are now 'using money wisely to send members of the Effective Learning Group to bring [ideas] back to the county'.

The school also has regular contact with the local authority. On the basic skills agenda, for example, there is a named contact who will investigate concerns raised by the schools. Thus the low linguistic ability of pupils in the current Year 7 will prompt an assessment of whether additional support is needed within the primary sector, or whether this simply happens to have been a weaker cohort. Engagement by local authority officers helps to ensure that, when they arise, concerns are dealt with promptly. Through the provision of opportunities for school representatives to come together and voice their opinions, the local authority also serves to connect Pembrokeshire's schools.

Members of the senior management team praised the 'constructive' relationship with the local authority and its 'family of schools'. Nevertheless, there remains one issue that is 'a tougher nut to crack'. This relates to the school's transition arrangements. Ysgol y Preseli does engage, through pastoral, pedagogic and data-sharing activities, with primary schools and their pupils prior to transition: pupils visit the school and are given taster lessons; the importance of bridging for linking KS1 and KS2 skills to KS3 is acknowledged; and under discussion are plans for a two-day induction programme for Year 7s, to cover the learning skills that will be used throughout the year, followed by a skills week in the summer term.

The school would, however, like to do more. Indeed, it has previously been able to do more, through the use of ring-fenced transition funding from the Welsh Government. This enabled teachers from the primary sector to visit Ysgol y Preseli, and vice versa, allowing each to better understand what happens on a daily basis in the other school. However, although that release continues to happen in the core subjects, following the end of the three-year funding cycle it is no longer as widespread. One respondent described the outcome thus:

> We were making really, really good progress with it. There's a programme still in place, but I think there was a momentum and that momentum has been lost.

The loss of funding has clearly complicated the school's transition arrangements, which are already less than straightforward given its wide catchment area. Fortunately, the headteachers of the seventeen primary schools that send pupils to Preseli have shown themselves to be happy to work with the school regardless of the availability of funding.

The squeeze on resources that is also affecting provision of learning support assistants in Ysgol y Preseli was described as 'a real threat' to the school's ability to continue adding substantial value at Key Stage 3. Ongoing efforts to increase the consistency of performance, through the sharing of the best possible practice within Preseli and with others within the local authority, must therefore be seen as an estimable means of cushioning the school against the damaging effects of further financial shocks.

Appendices

Appendix 1:
Project method

Two issues of research interest emerged from the statistics presented in Chapter 1 of this report. The first was that the period between KS2 and KS3 assessments, following pupils' transition to secondary school, appears to be one during which access to learning environments appropriate to each pupil's needs is far from equal. This has an attendant impact on performance. The second was that this inequality has not yet been reduced. Good practice, a notoriously bad traveller, would seem not be spreading to those schools with the least good KS3 results.

The Assembly's 2002 'Narrowing the Gap'[7] report notes that one of the most significant factors affecting a school's performance is the extent of its pupils' entitlement to free school meals (FSM). The link between deprivation and poor performance is a widely acknowledged one, in both policy[34] and academic[35] circles. The 2010 Estyn annual report finds that 'the gap between performance of disadvantaged and more advantaged learners ... has not closed' during the most recent inspection cycle[36]. However, as 'Narrowing the Gap' also finds, schools with similar levels of FSM entitlement can vary widely in their performance. It must therefore be the case that interventions are possible that will improve performance regardless of socioeconomic circumstance.

---

34   See, for example, Estyn, 2009, 'The impact of RAISE 2008-2009' and Estyn, 2010, 'Tackling child poverty and disadvantage in schools'.

35   This is discussed in relation to the Welsh case by D. Egan and S. Marshall in 'Educational leadership and school renewal in Wales', Australian Journal of Education 51(3): 286-298, 2007. See also T. Wendell, 2000, 'Creating equity and quality', Kelowna: SAEE for discussion of further research on this topic.

36   Estyn, 2010, 'Annual Report 2009-2010'.

Research questions

From these observations, three **research questions** emerged:

— What factors, both at a whole-school level and in relation to Key Stage 3, contribute to outstanding performance?
— How are these factors put into practice in different school environments?
— What lessons can be learnt from these findings by schools and by policy makers?

The first element of the focus here was on interventions at the level of the school or of groups of schools, up to and including the whole maintained sector. Consensus clearly suggests that the majority of variation in attainment can be accounted for by differences in socioeconomic status. Accordingly, policy aimed at targeting deprivation and social injustice can contribute significantly to raising KS3 attainment. However, there is also a case for understanding how certain schools are themselves able to buck the trend and raise attainment among deprived pupils.

Since deprivation, the most powerful factor in explaining differences in attainment, is a factor outside the control of schools, and given that this research focuses on school-level interventions, contextual value added data were used to select the case study schools. This had the effect of controlling for deprivation levels, and other variables that impact on performance, allowing the influence of the school to be more readily observed.

The second part of the research focused on understanding *in detail* how particular factors are operationalised within schools. Reports such as 'Aiming for Excellence in Key Stage 3'[37] and the follow-up 'Moving On...Improving Learning'[38] have attempted to provide guidance to schools on good practice. Nevertheless, it is not always clear what precisely might be required of a school, as for example when schools are urged to 'accelerate the rate of progress made by pupils'. This is most likely a goal shared by many, and yet the devil is undoubtedly in the detail. The 'what to do' of improving

---

37   Estyn, Welsh Assembly Government and ACCAC, 2002, 'Aiming for Excellence in Key Stage 3'.

38   Estyn, Welsh Assembly Government and ACCAC, 2004, 'Moving On...Improving Learning: Effective Transition from Key Stage 2 to Key Stage 3'.

performance is much discussed. This report seeks to present modest recommendations on 'how to do it'.

The research that underlies this report comprised three phases:

Phase I
Ranking and cross-referencing of all Welsh maintained schools according to KS2-KS3 Model 2a Contextual Value Added data for the three years 2006-2008.

Contextual value added data control for effects other than school effect on pupil performance. This allows the impact on performance of the school to be more accurately identified.

Using these data in combination with information on the date of each school's most recent Estyn inspection, from an initial list of 222 secondary schools thirty were chosen for further analysis in Phase II. These consisted of ten schools that have displayed significant positive added value in at least two of the three study years, ten that had KS3 outcomes not significantly different from those predicted, and ten that have produced results which are significantly worse than expected.

Phase II
Creation of a preliminary list of characteristics that constitute outstanding performance and contribute to added value at KS3.

Analysis of the thirty schools' most recent Estyn reports was undertaken. The reports were mined for evidence of factors contributing to high or low value added. Some of these factors are specific to KS3 and others impact at the whole-school level. Particular attention was paid to finding detailed descriptions of how good practice is operationalised in schools, in order to inform the questioning employed in Phase III.

Context for these findings was provided by reference to a range of academic and policy documents on school effectiveness. The preliminary findings of Phase II were also presented at the IWA's Learning Pathways conference in February 2010, so as to solicit the opinions of other experts in the field.

Phase III
Case study investigation of how outstanding features are put into practice within different school environments.

From the thirty schools studied in Phase II, five were selected for more detailed investigation. These schools demonstrated outstanding performance in one or more of the areas identified in Phase II. Semi-structured interviews were conducted with staff and students.

Recognising the limited utility of decontextualised lists of outstanding features, the end purpose of Phase III was to contextualise these features, giving a more detailed description of their implementation and the conditions under which they produce a positive effect.

Evolution of the project
The author's involvement with this project began at a time when a draft research proposal was already in existence. Subsequently, in response to the nature of the data available from the Welsh Government and to ensure that the later phases of the project yielded the best possible results, significant alterations were made to the project focus and method.

Initially, the work plan for Phase I was to acquire school-level data on pupil performance at Key Stage 3 and on free school meal (FSM) uptake for three consecutive years. The intention was to generate new three-year average figures, so as to reduce the impact of any anomalous data present in each year's results.

The school level was deemed the most appropriate firstly for reasons of expediency; to gain access to and analyse data at the pupil level would have been to introduce an additional time and resource requirement that would have made the research non-viable. Given that the research purpose is to understand how and why particular *schools* succeed in achieving good KS3 results regardless of intake, it was also determined that pupil-level data were less appropriate than school-level data.

Taking as a starting point the assumption that academic performance and socioeconomic status are correlated, KS3 performance and FSM uptake data were to have been used to identify schools that, according to this assumption, perform counter-intuitively. Six schools displaying such counter-intuitive outcomes would have been selected for detailed study, three from the top thirty and three from the bottom thirty schools, as ranked by KS3 performance.

However, discussions with the project steering group identified concerns with this methodological approach. Firstly, the focus on outlying schools – those displaying the most unlikely KS3 results as predicted by FSM entitlement – could have led to the distortion of findings. Since outliers are, by definition, those cases located furthest from the norm, the broader applicability of findings derived solely from their study could be called into question.

Secondly, in using statistics already aggregated to the level of each school cohort, at no stage would a direct match have been made between each pupil's attainment and his or her individual socioeconomic circumstances. FSM uptake would therefore have been being employed effectively as a school-level indicator of deprivation rather than a pupil-level indicator; attempts to correlate deprivation and performance would potentially have been clouded. To illustrate by example: a notional school with 30% FSM uptake produces far better KS3 results than a second school with similar uptake. Is the first school necessarily performing counter-intuitively? If the school is engaged in activities with that 30% to raise attainment, then the answer is most likely 'yes'. But perhaps the school is not intervening at all with its more deprived pupils, and the remaining 70% of pupils, who happen to come from particularly affluent homes, are positively skewing the results. In that case, on reflection the school looks to be performing far less counter-intuitively. What is hidden by such 'raw' scores is more adequately accounted for by using value added data, as described in Appendix 2.

Thirdly, the decision to identify poorly performing schools for further study in the final phase of the project was questioned. It was noted that obtaining cooperation from schools for the interview phase was more likely where the focus was on a school's achievements rather than its failings. In addition, it is considerably easier to identify what a school is specifically doing to add value than to second-guess what factors might, if introduced, lead to an improvement in performance.

The three-phase method described above was developed in response to these concerns. The process and outcomes of Phases II and III are set out in the main body of the report. Phase I, the statistical analysis underlying the qualitative research, is described in Appendix 2.

Appendix 2:
Differentiation of schools using CVA data

The availability of pupil-matched KS2-KS3 contextual value added data, aggregated to the school level, facilitated the application of an alternative method to that initially envisaged (see Appendix 1). The Welsh Government produces a range of value added data; this includes Simple Value Added (VA), which compares each pupil's current attainment with prior attainment, and Contextual Value Added (CVA). These measures are calculated using the Core Subject Indicator (CSI), which measures pupils' achievement of the expected level in the core subjects of English or Welsh, mathematics and science.

In comparing current with prior attainment, the CVA Model 2a data obtained by the Institute take account of the impact on performance of the following factors:

— Free school meal entitlement, at the pupil level
— Two school-level deprivation factors:
    – Welsh Index of Multiple Deprivation
    – Acorn geodemographic data
— Pupil age in months
— Pupil gender
— Pupil ethnicity
— Two pupil mobility factors:
    – Whether pupil started in a new school at the beginning of the academic year
    – Length of time at current school

Actual pupil performance is compared with the performance predicted according to the above model. Because each of the above factors has been controlled for, the difference between these two scores shows the value that has been added by the school. By analysing school-level CVA data it is therefore possible to identify schools that are consistently adding genuine value, as distinct from those that simply achieve high marks at KS3.

The model matches each factor at the pupil level, ensuring that the value added data, whilst aggregated here to the school level, are accurately correlated at the pupil level. Had straightforward mapping of aggregated FSM uptake against results data been undertaken, this nuance would have been lost: only whole-cohort performance against whole-cohort FSM uptake would have been charted, with no reference to individuals' performance relative to their own personal socioeconomic characteristics.

Contextual value added figures derive from analysis conducted on pupil-level data, and are only subsequently aggregated to the school level. Using these data has therefore allowed the Institute to draw on a more detailed understanding of school performance than would have been possible through a straightforward exercise mapping attainment against FSM uptake. It also serves to ensure that schools are placed on a relatively level playing field for the purposes of comparison.

Having obtained KS2-KS3 CVA data for all maintained schools in Wales for the last three available years (2006-2008), the schools were ranked according to their value added scores. This was carried out separately for each year's data since, given the nature of value added scores, it would be meaningless to average the data across the three years. (If, for instance, a school obtains CVA scores of 13.0, 0 and -13.0 over three years, the average would be 0. This average would give no indication of the fact that in the first year 13% more pupils than expected achieved the CSI, whereas in the third year 13% fewer pupils than expected did so.)

The fifty schools in each year with the highest value added were then cross-referenced to find schools that appeared in at least two of the years. This highlighted schools demonstrating some degree of consistency in adding value during the study years. Although in any one year some schools with statistically significant value added, at the 95% significance level, fell outside the fifty school cut-off point, this point minimised the inclusion of schools with non-significant value added scores. At the same time it ensured a broad sample within which to find reoccurring schools. The process was repeated for the fifty schools with the most negative value added scores. Cross-referencing was also undertaken on a sample of schools displaying no statistically significant added value; this sample included schools within twenty-five places above and below the median value added score.

From an initial list of 222 maintained schools, thirty-eight were highlighted as producing consistently high value added, twenty-six 'added' negative value and thirty-two consistently performed as expected. These 96 schools were further narrowed down to 58 through the elimination of schools without an Estyn inspection report for 2006 or later. The Phase II analysis of factors leading to outstanding performance was based on Estyn reports, and was reliant on identification of differences between schools from right across the performance spectrum. Only by using inspection reports for the same time period as that covered by the CVA data could we be certain that the assessment of performance contained in those reports matched the analysis provided by the CVA figures, and thus that a full range of schools was being studied.

Of these 58 schools, ten were selected for further study from each of the categories of 'positive', 'negative' and 'zero' value added. To select the final thirty, all schools appearing in their respective category for three consecutive years were chosen. The remaining places were filled following advice from Estyn on schools of potential interest – including those requiring special measures or significant improvement and those with outstanding features – and by taking account of the need to include a range of schools based on geographical, religious and linguistic characteristics.